VEGETABLE CREATIONS

Complete Gardener's Library™

NATIONAL HOME
GARDENING CLUB

CREDITS

About the Author

Mary Evans, founder of *Mary Evans Cooks*, has been involved in the culinary field for the past 20 years. A former cooking school director, she enjoys sharing her passion for food with others through cooking classes, developing recipes, and writing on a wide variety of food topics. Addicted to travel, she leads food-related tours in the U.S. and France. Her culinary background involves studies at La Varenne and Lenôtre. Mary is a member of the International Association of Culinary Professionals and Les Dames d'Escoffier.

VEGETABLE CREATIONS

Printed in 2005.

Tom Carpenter, Creative Director
Jennifer Guinea, Senior Book Development Coordinator
Tad Ware & Company: Book Design and Production
Photography
Food Styling
Recipe Testing

On Cover: Fresh Tomato Salad with Pesto Croutons, page 44.

1 2 3 4 5 6 7 8 / 08 07 06 05
© 2005 National Home Gardening Club
ISBN 1-58159-247-7

National Home Gardening Club
12301 Whitewater Drive
Minnetonka, MN 55343
www.gardeningclub.com

TABLE OF CONTENTS

*I*NTRODUCTION

Let's play word association. Describe vegetables. What's the first word that comes to mind — colorful, flavorful, delicious, crunchy,  healthy? Carry those words with you the next time you work in your garden, visit the produce section of your supermarket or attend your local farmers' market. Notice the vivid palette of colors glowing back at you. Feel the endless variety of textures that vegetables represent — from smooth to velvety, from firm to reply yielding. Your enjoyment has begun and you haven't even picked anything or made a purchase!

Now try this. Don't think about vegetables as something to fill up the holes on your plate. Instead, move them center stage and think of everything else as complementary. Many of the recipes in this book make vegetables the star of any course. You'll find an excellent assortment of appetizers, soups, main dishes and desserts, along with the more typical salads and side dishes. According to most health studies, eating vegetables contributes significantly to longevity; experts suggest three to five vegetable servings per day. Make produce the focus of your diet and you'll be amazed how great you feel.

What's more, if you grow your own vegetables — as many National Home Gardening Club Members do — you get the double benefit of all that gardening activity. It's good for your heart (literally) … and your soul.

But even beyond fabulous recipes utilizing a bounty of vegetable gardens, this book includes a section on cooking techniques for recipe success, with broader suggestions for adding life to any vegetable side dish. Check out some of the tools and gadgets that make cooking easier. The glossary sums up all the useful, factual information you need to know about vegetables; it also offers tips on how to select the best and freshest produce, and how to keep your vegetables at optimum quality once you've harvested them or brought them home.

Yes, vegetables add beautiful color, vibrant flavor, pleasurable crunch and essential nutrients to your diet. Whether you grow your own or buy them market fresh, vegetables are to be celebrated and savored. That's what *Vegetable Creations* is all about.

Techniques & Tools

Vegetables respond well to many different cooking techniques. But sometimes it's not clear just what all the technical terms mean, or how they're actually executed. Use these guidelines with the recipes that follow; if you're adventuresome, these guidelines can help you create your own wonderful dishes from vegetables.

Blanching or parboiling involves dropping vegetables into a large quantity of rapidly boiling water for a short period of time. It is meant to partially, but not completely, cook the food being blanched.

There are several reasons to blanch. Sometimes cooks use this technique to set the color of a vegetable or make it more vivid. For example, the pea pods in *Spicy Pea Pod and Orange Salad* (page 55) take on fabulous color after their brief plunge in boiling water. Sometimes vegetables are blanched to make them more tender, as are the sugar snaps and asparagus in *Spring Sugar Snaps, Asparagus Spears and Radishes with Mint-Chive Dip* (page 39).

Try blanching or parboiling sometime when adding a vegetable such as broccoli to a salad, to make it more colorful and tender. Blanching is also necessary before freezing vegetables to retard enzyme action.

After blanching, drain vegetables and then, if small quantities are involved, run under cold water to avoid overcooking. For larger quantities, have a bowl of water with ice handy and plunge the drained, blanched vegetables into it.

BRAISE/STEW

Braising is a term that describes the process of cooking a particular food slowly in a small amount of liquid. Stewing usually involves more than one food item, and often calls for more liquid.

These similar techniques use a covered or partially covered pot on top of the stove, in the oven or in a slow cooker. Cook food in this manner to either tenderize, add moisture or mingle flavors. Some examples are the *Braised Beans in Hoisin Sauce* (page 80), *Cauliflower and Garbanzo Bean Tagine* (page 105), *Indian Root Vegetable Curry* (page 109) and *Vegetarian Gumbo* (page 117), among others.

Also use these techniques when cooking tougher, leaner cuts of meats (with or without vegetables), or any time you want flavors to blend.

These techniques involve cooking food above or below a direct heat source. Both grilling and broiling produce similar results — quickly cooked food that is well-browned.

Because this is a dry cooking process, vegetables need to be brushed or sprayed with a bit of oil to keep them from losing their moisture while cooking. Grilled or broiled vegetables develop a slightly smoky or charred taste that complements certain dishes. Because the heat source is so intense, watch food carefully to avoid burning. Food should not be too thick or large when prepared in this manner or else it will not cook properly.

The recipe for *Black Bean, Corn and Green Chile Quesadillas* (page 25) cooks both the corn and the chiles in this way. Also try grilling or broiling for vegetables to serve with pasta or on top of pizza: Cut the vegetables into slices, cook until well-browned and cut into bite-size pieces.

$\mathcal{M}$ICROWAVE

In general, vegetables cook very well in the microwave. Microwaves cook by moving the water molecules around in food, creating friction and thus generating heat. Most vegetables have a high moisture content and thus cook quickly and well. The resulting texture will be similar to steamed foods.

Because this technique requires little or no additional liquid, water-soluble vitamins are not washed away during the cooking process. While microwaving is not specified in any of the recipes in this book, try it when cooked vegetables are listed as ingredients. Corn, winter squash and sweet potatoes would be prime examples.

Because microwaves vary widely in wattages, refer to your owner's manual for proper cooking times. Do not microwave vegetables when browning is desired.

ROAST

Roasting is a dry heat process that involves cooking food in the oven, using fairly high heat to promote browning. Although it is most often used for meats, roasting also caramelizes vegetables and gives them a richer taste. Roasting is used in the recipe for *Rich Vegetable Stock* (page 61).

Here's another idea. Try cutting up vegetables (most any will do), toss them with a bit of oil and place them in a fairly hot oven (400°F or so) for 30 to 45 minutes, stirring occasionally. Cut the larger vegetables into chunks before roasting. Serve these flavorful vegetables as a no-fuss side dish with lots of taste.

$\mathcal{S}$AUTE/STIR-FRY

Both sautéing and stir-frying cook food quickly over a direct heat source, using a large cooking surface and a small amount of oil or fat.

Sautéing involves a skillet and is usually done over medium to medium-high heat. It takes a bit longer than stir-frying. Onion and garlic are often sautéed at the beginning of a recipe to quickly soften them and release their flavor.

Stir-fry in a wok over high heat; position the wok as close to the heat source as possible. Because the outer surface of food is cooked so quickly, it needs to be chopped, cut in strips or be relatively thin so that the interior will cook before the exterior burns. *Sesame Asparagus* (page 90) is a good example of wok cooking.

Use the stir-fry method for an easy, quick dinner. Here's how: Cut whatever vegetables you have on hand into strips. Do the same with a small amount of meat, if desired. Stir-fry the vegetables with a bit of oil, ginger and garlic; start by adding the vegetables that are a bit sturdier and need more cooking. Add a little water, if necessary, to finish the process by steaming. If adding meat, remove the vegetables, add a little more oil and quickly stir-fry the meat. Return the vegetables to the pan, adding a bit of bottled stir-fry sauce or oyster or hoisin sauce for flavor. Serve with rice.

SIMMER/BOIL

Simmering involves heating liquid until small bubbles form; boiling creates larger bubbles. Use low heat when simmering, medium heat or higher for boiling.

Because simmering is a gentler, slower cooking method, it is often used to avoid breaking apart food, and to concentrate taste. Soups are often simmered to release flavors into the cooking liquid. Broths and stocks do the same while evaporating some of the liquid to intensify the final product. Both stock recipes in this book rely on simmering, as do most of the soups.

Boiling cooks food more rapidly without releasing flavors. The green beans in *Green Beans Provencal* (page 83) are initially cooked this way. Sweet corn also cooks very well by boiling. Another advantage of boiling is that a large quantity of vegetables can be cooked very quickly.

$\mathcal{S}$TEAM

Steaming involves placing vegetables in a basket or insert with holes, then positioning the basket above a small amount of boiling water in a pan. The pan is covered and the resulting steam cooks the vegetables. Because the vegetables do not come in direct contact with the water, flavor and water-soluble vitamins are retained.

This technique is best for cooking relatively small amounts of vegetables simply and quickly. This is an easy way to cook vegetables simply for side dishes. Use this method to cook an accompaniment to an elaborate dish, for example, where anything but a plain vegetable would compete for attention.

USEFUL TOOLS

A good tool is an enormous asset for any kind of endeavor. Cooking is no exception. Here's a list of important tools and gadgets designed to make your vegetable creations even better, and your life in the kitchen easier.

ELECTRIC VEGETABLE JUICERS

These devices turn solid pieces of vegetables and fruits into juices quickly and easily. Look for sturdy, well-constructed models from reputable manufacturers.

FOOD PROCESSORS AND BLENDERS

Both food processors and blenders are electrical devices designed to puree food. Food processors also come with blades designed for slicing and shredding. Look for sturdy models with good motors.

POTATO MASHER

This device has a long handle and flattened base to mash cooked potatoes. The base, usually made of metal, is either bent into parallel U shapes or else made with many holes. The potatoes are crushed by the base and broken into a thick, fluffy mass. Another device used to make mashed potatoes is a potato ricer. A pushing section forces potatoes through small holes in the bottom of the ricer.

GARLIC PRESS

There are several styles of garlic presses available, but a good press should allow the user to force the garlic through the holes without much trouble. It should fit comfortably in the hand and clean without too much effort. You may want to look for a brand that comes with a reverse grid to press any remaining garlic out of the holes to aid in cleaning. In addition, you want to choose a press that is designed with an ergonomic grip. It may take some experimentation to find the press that works best for you.

VEGETABLE PEELER

This small tool becomes a lifesaver when you are faced with a mountain of potatoes for Thanksgiving, but will be appreciated for small jobs too. There are different styles available. Some models have the blade running in a straight line from the handle, others position the blade perpendicularly. The better styles have a swivel blade that compensates for the irregular surface of the vegetable being peeled. Some come with ergonomic grips. Experiment to find out which one suits you best. Discard peelers that have grown dull.

KNIVES

What makes a good knife? The best knives are often made of a combination of stainless and carbon steel, allowing for ease in sharpening while eliminating rust. Good knives have a piece of metal (called the tang) that extends from the blade down the length of the handle. This tang is attached by rivets. There are a variety of knives available to perform specific cutting tasks, but the knife best suited for such things as slicing, dicing and chopping is a chef's knife.

This chef's knife is extremely useful for slicing and chopping because of its elongated, triangular shape. Chef's knives come in several lengths; try to decide which length will be most comfortable for you and, if possible, see how it feels in your hand before purchase. Another useful knife is a small paring knife. It is very efficient for peeling, paring and other cutting jobs that involve smaller pieces of food. Asian chefs prefer using a cleaver, a hatchet-shaped knife that easily cuts through vegetables and meats.

Italian cooks sometimes use a mezzaluna, a curved blade with handles on both ends. The blade chops and minces by rocking back and forth over food on a cutting board or in a rounded bowl.

MANDOLINES AND SLICERS

Mandolines are hand-operated, nonelectrical devices used for slicing and cutting vegetables into various sized strips. These tools have adjustable blades to allow for slicing and cutting in different thicknesses. The classic French mandoline is metal, but there are various plastic models available, some of which also shred and grate. An older American variation on this idea is the Feemster slicer, a simple device used for slicing. Protective guards

should be used to prevent cutting yourself. If protective guards aren't available, wear an oven mitt on the hand gripping the food you are slicing.

POTS AND PANS

Good quality pots and pans should be relatively heavy and conduct heat evenly. Certain metals — such as aluminum, copper and cast iron — conduct heat better than others. All of these metals can react with foods and are often sold with coatings or sealed in some way. Aluminum and cast iron can cause off-flavors or discoloration when used with certain foods, and copper generally needs to be lined with another metal for food safety reasons. Therefore, aluminum often comes sealed with a protective surface or combined in some way with stainless steel. Stainless steel is, by itself, a poor heat conductor and is usually combined with another metal. It contributes durability and does not react with foods. Cast iron is sometimes coated with enamel. Whether or not to use nonstick surfaces is another consideration. Food tends to brown better in a regular skillet, but nonstick aids significantly in cleanup.

STEAMER INSERTS

The insert is placed inside a large pot that contains a small amount of water; the base has legs that keep the bottom out of the water. The collapsible side panels are expanded to form a basket, and vegetables are added. The water is brought to a boil and the pot is covered. The vegetables are steamed through holes in the bottom and sides of the insert. These inserts come in smaller and larger sizes to fit a variety of pots and pans.

TIPS FOR TASTE

TIPS FOR TASTE

To jazz up vegetable side dishes, herbs are a great addition. Basil, dill, tarragon, thyme and many others go well with many vegetables.

Citrus is another easy flavor booster. A splash of lemon or a bit of orange or lime zest makes a dish taste fabulous with no effort.

Spicy seasonings add lots of zing too.

Nuts add crunch, and butter or olive oil makes everything taste better.

Sprinkle a bit of crumbled bacon or cheese over vegetables for another flavor boost.

Bottled sauces and spice blends can add flavor and zest to simple vegetable dishes when time is short.

Try different ethnic seasonings such as Thai or Indian for a change of pace.

Substitute different vegetables for the ones called for in recipes. Go ahead! For instance, if you don't have asparagus, try broccoli in the *Sesame Asparagus* (page 90) recipe.

Cooking is a creative process. Let your imagination and seasonal availability guide you to make cooking more pleasurable and eating a delight.

BEVERAGES & APPETIZERS

Try the two tempting juice recipes here as beverage options the next time you are entertaining. Along with the versatile selection of appetizers, they're a guaranteed hit. From easy to elegant, these thirst-quenchers and nibblers present plenty of afternoon pick-me-up options too.

Frosty Mary, page 24
Black Bean, Corn and Green Chile Quesadillas, page 25

FROSTY MARY

If a juicer is unavailable, use 1 quart of a purchased tomato-based vegetable juice. Freeze 2 cups with vodka and seasonings, omitting salt, and stir the slush mixture into the remaining 2 cups of juice the next day.

- 4 medium tomatoes
- 8 medium carrots
- 4 large ribs celery
- 1/2 cup vodka
- 1 teaspoon salt
- 1/4 teaspoon freshly ground pepper
- 1/4 teaspoon hot pepper sauce
- 1/4 teaspoon grated horseradish, if desired

❶ The day before serving, juice 2 tomatoes, 4 carrots and 2 ribs celery in an electric vegetable juicer according to manufacturer's directions. Place in plastic container along with vodka, salt, pepper, hot pepper sauce and horseradish. Stir to combine. Freeze overnight, covered.

❷ When ready to serve, juice remaining tomatoes, carrots and celery. Using tines of fork, break up frozen mixture into icy shreds; stir into juice or pulse in blender to combine. Divide evenly among 4 glasses. Garnish with celery, if desired. To make a nonalcoholic variation, simply omit the vodka. Do not freeze, but serve as juice.

4 servings.
Preparation time: 15 minutes. Ready to serve: 8 hours, 15 minutes.
Per serving: 165 calories, 1 g total fat (0 g saturated fat), 0 mg cholesterol, 700 mg sodium, 1.5 g fiber.

BLACK BEAN, CORN AND GREEN CHILE QUESADILLAS

Serve these quesadillas while relaxing on your patio on a perfect summer evening. If using a skillet on the grill to finish the quesadillas, make sure the handle is heat-resistant. Otherwise, finish them on the cooktop inside.

2	medium ears corn
2	Anaheim or New Mexico chiles
1	(15-oz.) can black beans, rinsed, drained
1/4	cup thinly sliced green onions
1	red jalapeño pepper, seeded, minced
1	tablespoon lime juice
1/2	teaspoon salt
4	(10-inch) flour tortillas
2	cups (8 oz.) shredded Monterey Jack cheese

❶ Remove silk from corn, leaving husks intact. Place corn and chiles on gas grill over medium-high heat or on charcoal grill 4 to 6 inches from medium-high coals. Grill chiles 8 to 10 minutes, turning when first side is charred. Grill corn about 12 minutes, turning 1/4 turn every 3 minutes.

❷ Remove chiles from heat; place in paper bag 5 minutes to loosen blackened skin. Remove corn from heat; let cool. Husk; remove kernels from cob. Place in medium bowl. Scrape skin from chiles; remove seeds and inner membranes. Chop chiles and place in bowl.

❸ Add black beans, onions, jalapeño, lime juice and salt. Divide mixture evenly among tortillas; spread on one half of each tortilla. Sprinkle each filled half with 1/2 cup of the cheese. Fold tortilla over filling.

❹ Heat large skillet or griddle on gas grill over medium-high heat or on charcoal grill 4 to 6 inches from medium-high coals, or on stove over medium-high heat. Cook each tortilla 4 minutes per side or until browned, turning once. Cut into quarters; serve with salsa, if desired.

8 servings.
Preparation time: 15 minutes. Ready to serve: 47 minutes.
Per serving: 290 calories, 11.5 g total fat (6 g saturated fat), 25 mg cholesterol, 570 mg sodium, 4.5 g fiber.

SCALLION AND CILANTRO POT STICKERS

Look for wonton skins in the produce or Asian section of large supermarkets, or in specialty food stores.

4	tablespoons vegetable oil
1	tablespoon chopped fresh ginger
1	cup chopped green onions, including tender green portion of stem
2½	cups chopped Savoy or Napa cabbage
2	tablespoons soy sauce
⅓	cup chopped cilantro
1½	teaspoons toasted sesame oil
24	wonton skins
⅔	cup water

❶ Heat 2 tablespoons of the vegetable oil in large nonstick skillet over high heat until hot. Add ginger; sauté 30 to 60 seconds or until fragrant. Add onions; sauté 2 to 3 minutes to soften slightly. Add cabbage and soy sauce; sauté 3 to 4 minutes or until cabbage is wilted and most of moisture is evaporated. Remove from heat; stir in cilantro and sesame oil. Place in medium bowl; cool.

❷ In center of each skin, place heaping teaspoonful of cabbage mixture. Moisten edges of skin with water. Fold skin in half to form half-moon shape. Pinch and pleat top layer of skin along rounded edge. Press edges of skin together to seal.

❸ Heat 1 tablespoon of the vegetable oil in large nonstick skillet over high heat until hot. Reduce heat to medium-high; add half of pot stickers, unfluted side down. Cook 2 to 3 minutes or until lightly browned on bottom. Add ⅓ cup of the water; cover and steam 3 to 4 minutes. Remove cover; cook an additional 1 to 2 minutes or until pot stickers are deep brown on bottom. Remove from skillet and repeat process, using remaining 1 tablespoon vegetable oil and ⅓ cup water to cook second half of pot stickers. Serve with citrus-soy dipping sauce.*

TIP *To make citrus-soy dipping sauce, see recipe for *Spring Rolls* (page 31).

24 pot stickers.
Preparation time: 40 minutes. Ready to serve: 52 minutes.
Per sticker: 60 calories, 4 g total fat (.5 g saturated fat), 5 mg cholesterol, 265 mg sodium, .5 g fiber.

JAZZED-UP JUICE

Try this peppy juice for a healthy, thirst-quenching beverage. If you don't have a juicer, combine 2/3 cup canned carrot juice with 1/3 cup apple juice for a tasty introduction to what juicing is all about.

- 4 medium carrots
- 2 large ribs celery
- 1 jalapeño pepper, seeded

❶ In electric vegetable juicer, process carrots, celery and jalapeño according to manufacturer's directions.

2¹/2 servings.

Preparation time: 5 minutes. Ready to serve: 5 minutes.

Per serving: 65 calories, .5 g total fat (0 g saturated fat), 0 mg cholesterol, 85 mg sodium, 1 g fiber.

GREAT GARLICKY DIP WITH SUMMER VEGETABLES

Roasted garlic is much milder than raw, and it is a perfect complement to the beans and olive oil in this flavorful dip. Try using the dip as a spread for sandwiches too.

1   large head garlic
2   tablespoons plus 1/2 teaspoon extra-virgin olive oil
1   tablespoon water
1   (15-oz.) can cannellini beans, rinsed, drained
1   tablespoon lemon juice
1/2 teaspoon salt
    Dash ground red pepper
6   cups assorted summer vegetables (cherry tomatoes, blanched
      green beans, zucchini spears, baby carrots, pattypan squash)
      cut into pieces

❶ Heat oven to 350°F. Remove outer papery skin of garlic. Cut pointed top of garlic to expose flesh. Place in center of 12-inch square piece of foil; drizzle with 1/2 teaspoon of the olive oil. Pull up edges of foil to form pouch; add water. Tighten edge of foil to seal; place in oven. Bake about 1 hour or until garlic is soft. Remove; let cool.

❷ Squeeze flesh of garlic from skin into bowl of food processor. Add beans; pulse to puree. Add remaining 2 tablespoons oil, lemon juice, salt and red pepper; pulse to combine. Place in small bowl; cover and refrigerate several hours to infuse flavors. Serve with vegetables.

12 servings.
Preparation time: 15 minutes. Ready to serve: 4 hours, 5 minutes.

Per serving: 75 calories, 2.5 g total fat (.5 g saturated fat), 0 mg cholesterol, 165 mg sodium, 3.5 g fiber.

SPRING ROLLS

Unlike fried spring rolls, these fresh rolls let the true flavor of the ingredients shine through. Look for the wrappers, sometimes called rice paper wrappers, in Asian markets or in large supermarkets.

FILLING

- 1 oz. bean thread noodles
- 1 cup shredded carrots
- 1/2 cup matchstick-size strips cucumber
- 1/2 cup whole fresh cilantro
- 1/4 cup slivered green onions
- 1/4 cup shredded turnip
- 1/4 cup chopped peanuts
- 2 tablespoons coarsely chopped fresh basil
- 2 tablespoons coarsely chopped fresh mint
- 1/2 jalapeño pepper, slivered
- 1/4 teaspoon salt
- 8 dried spring roll wrappers

DIPPING SAUCE

- 1/4 cup soy sauce
- 1/4 cup orange juice
- 1/4 cup water
- 2 tablespoons white or red wine vinegar
- 2 tablespoons slivered green onion
- 1 teaspoon grated orange peel

❶ Place noodles in medium bowl; cover with boiling water. Soak 15 minutes. Drain; cut into 1-inch pieces.

❷ In large bowl, combine noodles, carrots, cucumber, cilantro, onion, turnip, peanuts, basil, mint, jalapeño and salt. In shallow dish, soak each wrapper in hot water until soft. Drain on towel. Place 1/8 of mixture on lower edge of each wrapper. Shape into tight cylinder by folding curved bottom edge up and over to enclose filling in one tight turn. Fold both outside edges inward to enclose filling at both ends. Continue rolling into packed cylinder. Cut in half diagonally.

❸ In small bowl, combine soy sauce, orange juice, water, vinegar, green onion and grated peel. Serve with Spring Rolls.

8 servings. Preparation time: 30 minutes. Ready to serve: 30 minutes.

Per serving: 80 calories, 2.5 g total fat (.5 g saturated fat), 5 mg cholesterol, 600 mg sodium, 1.5 g fiber.

SPINACH PESTO-STUFFED MUSHROOMS

The bread crumbs in the mixture absorb excess moisture from the spinach and mushrooms. To cut back on oil, try spraying the mushroom caps with olive oil-flavored nonstick cooking spray instead of brushing them with olive oil.

1 large garlic clove
2 cups coarsely chopped fresh spinach
1/2 cup coarsely chopped fresh basil
1/3 cup dry bread crumbs
1/4 cup (1 oz.) freshly grated Parmesan cheese
5 tablespoons extra-virgin olive oil
1 lb. medium mushrooms (32 to 36 mushrooms), stems removed

❶ Heat oven to 400°F. With motor running, drop garlic clove into bowl of food processor to chop. Add spinach and basil; pulse until very finely chopped. Add bread crumbs and cheese; pulse to combine. With motor running, add 3 tablespoons of the oil to form thick paste.

❷ Brush mushroom caps with remaining 2 tablespoons oil; place on shallow baking sheet. Fill each cap with about 1 teaspoon filling, pressing into cavity and mounding on top. Bake 15 to 20 minutes or until mushrooms are tender and filling is hot.

32 to 36 mushrooms.
Preparation time: 15 minutes. Ready to serve: 30 minutes.

Per mushroom: 30 calories, 2.5 g total fat (.5 g saturated fat), 0 mg cholesterol, 30 mg sodium, .5 g fiber.

SOUTHWESTERN ROASTED PUMPKIN SEEDS

Raw pepitas are pumpkin seeds used in Mexican cooking. They can be found in health food stores, supermarkets or Hispanic grocery stores. If unavailable, substitute your favorite raw nut.

2   tablespoons vegetable oil
1   tablespoon chili powder
1   teaspoon cider vinegar
1   teaspoon garlic salt
1/2 teaspoon ground cumin
1/2 teaspoon cayenne
1/4 teaspoon salt
2   cups raw pepitas

❶ Heat oven to 350°F. In medium bowl, combine oil, chili powder, vinegar, garlic salt, cumin, cayenne and salt. Stir to combine. Add pepitas; stir to coat. Spread on 15x10x1-inch pan. Bake 10 to 15 minutes, or until browned and crisp, stirring every 5 minutes. Remove from oven; cool. Scrape pepitas and seasonings into bowl; stir briefly.

8 servings.
Preparation time: 5 minutes. Ready to serve: 15 minutes.

Per serving: 215 calories, 18 g total fat (3.5 g saturated fat), 0 mg cholesterol, 210 mg sodium, 2.5 g fiber.

TEX-MEX POTATO SKINS

These spicy appetizers are perfect while watching a football game or for casual entertaining. The pepper Jack cheese adds extra heat. If not available, seed and chop two jalapeño peppers and sprinkle over 4 ounces of Monterey Jack cheese.

4	medium-large russet potatoes
1/2	teaspoon garlic salt
2	oz. shredded cheddar cheese
2	oz. shredded pepper Jack cheese
1/2	cup sour cream
1	cup medium-chunky salsa
1/2	cup sliced green onion tops

❶ Heat oven to 400°F. Prick potatoes in several places with fork or tip of knife; bake on baking sheet at 400°F for about 1¼ to 1½ hours, or until slightly overdone (skins should be crispy and firm). Let cool on wire rack; cut into quarters. With spoon, remove most of flesh. Reduce oven temperature to 350°F.

❷ Line 2 baking sheets with aluminum foil or parchment paper. Place potato skins on baking sheets, flesh side up. Sprinkle lightly with salt. In medium bowl, combine cheddar and pepper Jack cheese; top each potato skin with 2 tablespoons cheese mixture. Bake potato skins at 350°F for 5 to 8 minutes or until cheese is melted.

❸ Top each potato skin with 1 tablespoon of the sour cream; drizzle each with salsa. Sprinkle with onions.

8 servings.
Preparation time: 10 minutes. Ready to serve: 1 hour, 30 minutes.

Per serving: 145 calories, 7.5 g total fat (4.5 g saturated fat), 25 mg cholesterol, 240 mg sodium, 1.5 g fiber.

VEGETARIAN FONDUE

Double this recipe and use it as a relaxing main course. Emmentaler cheese is the real thing — cheese from Switzerland with holes throughout. You may substitute Swiss Gruyère or another high-quality imported Swiss-style cheese.

1	tablespoon cornstarch
1/4	teaspoon dry ground mustard
1	cup plus 2 tablespoons white wine
1	whole clove garlic, peeled, slightly crushed
12	oz. Emmentaler cheese, cut into 1/4-inch cubes
	Dash ground nutmeg
	Hearty rye bread loaf, cut into 1-inch cubes
	Vegetables of your choice

1 In small bowl, combine cornstarch and dry mustard; mix well. Add 2 tablespoons wine; stir to combine. Set aside.

2 Heat 1 cup wine and garlic in medium saucepan over low heat until bubbles begin to appear around edges of wine. Remove garlic. Add cheese and nutmeg; stir until cheese begins to melt. Stir in cornstarch mixture; continue to cook about 5 minutes or until mixture begins to thicken, stirring constantly. Pour into fondue pot or heat-proof serving dish; set over flame. Serve with bread, and your choice of broccoli, cauliflower and eggplant.

8 servings.
Preparation time: 15 minutes. Ready to serve: 20 minutes.

Per serving: 200 calories, 12 g total fat (7.5 g saturated fat), 40 mg cholesterol, 175 mg sodium, 1.5 g fiber.

CARAMELIZED ONION AND GOAT CHEESE PHYLLO TRIANGLES

Look for phyllo dough in the freezer section of the grocery store. Before using, thaw in the refrigerator 6 to 8 hours or overnight. While working with one sheet, cover the others with a barely dampened towel to keep them from drying out. Wrap unused phyllo tightly and refreeze for later use.

2	tablespoons vegetable oil
2	medium onions, thinly sliced
1/2	teaspoon sugar
1/2	teaspoon dried thyme
1/4	teaspoon salt
1/8	teaspoon freshly ground pepper
1	(3.5- to 4-oz.) package goat cheese
4	(14 x 18-inch) sheets frozen phyllo, thawed
5	tablespoons butter, melted

❶ Heat oil in large skillet over medium heat until hot. Add onions; sauté onions about 5 minutes, or until slightly softened, stirring occasionally. Reduce heat to low; cover and cook 5 minutes, stirring occasionally. Uncover; add sugar. Cook an additional 10 to 15 minutes or until onions are very soft and golden brown. Add thyme, salt and pepper; mix well. Remove from heat. Let cool. Stir in goat cheese.

❷ Heat oven to 400°F. Place 1 sheet of phyllo on cutting board; brush with butter. Cut into 8 (2¼ x 14-inch) strips. Place 1 teaspoon goat cheese mixture in lower right corner of each strip. Fold corners up and over to enclose filling, forming a triangle. Continue each strip and fold one corner to opposite side to form triangle. Continue to fold, triangle fashion, up length of strip. Brush with melted butter; place on ungreased baking sheet. Repeat with remaining strips, and remaining 3 sheets phyllo.

❸ Bake 10 to 12 minutes or until phyllo triangles are browned and crisp. Serve warm or room temperature.

32 triangles. Preparation time: 50 minutes. Ready to serve: 1 hour.

Per triangle: 48 calories, 4 g total fat (2 g saturated fat), 10 mg cholesterol, 50 mg sodium, 0 g fiber.

SPRING SUGAR SNAPS, ASPARAGUS SPEARS AND RADISHES WITH MINT-CHIVE DIP

This recipe uses spring's wonderful produce and herbs to make a delightful hors d'oeuvre. To prepare asparagus, hold the spear with two hands, bend slightly and snap off the unyielding portion at the end. If the skin seems tough, remove with a vegetable peeler. Submerge in water and swirl spears to remove any grit lodged in the tips.

3/4   lb. sugar snap peas
3/4   lb. asparagus spears, trimmed, cut into 2 1/2-inch pieces
1/2   lb. radishes

DIP
1   cup sour cream
2   tablespoons chopped fresh mint
2   tablespoons chopped fresh chives
1/4   teaspoon salt
1/8   teaspoon freshly ground pepper

❶ Fill large saucepan half full with water. Bring to a boil over high heat; add peas and asparagus. Cook 2 minutes. Drain; run peas and asparagus under cold water to stop cooking. Cover; set aside until ready to serve.

❷ In small bowl, combine sour cream, mint, chives, salt and pepper. Serve with peas, asparagus and radishes.

8 servings.
Preparation time: 20 minutes. Ready to serve: 20 minutes.

Per serving: 90 calories, 6 g total fat (3.5 g saturated fat), 20 mg cholesterol, 95 mg sodium, 2.5 g fiber.

SALADS

There's something refreshingly satisfying about a salad. The cool crunch of crisp lettuce paired with tangy dressing brings taste buds alive with each bite. Versatile in nature, salads welcome a variety of produce plus such diverse additions as bread or grains. Make up your own combinations! And try different vinegars and oils for endless dressing possibilities.

Beet, Apple and Gruyère Salad, page 42

BEET, APPLE AND GRUYERE SALAD

If available, try substituting yellow or candy cane striped beets for the red variety. Make sure to add the beets first, before the apples or cheese, to keep their vivid colors separate from the other ingredients.

VINAIGRETTE
- 2 tablespoons cider vinegar
- 1½ teaspoons Dijon mustard
- ½ cup vegetable oil
- 1½ teaspoons chopped fresh tarragon or ½ teaspoon dried
- ⅛ teaspoon salt
  Pinch freshly ground pepper

SALAD
- 1 large or 2 small cooked beets, peeled, thinly sliced*
- 1 large Granny Smith apple, thinly sliced
- 8 cups bite-size pieces romaine lettuce and arugula
- 4 oz. Gruyère cheese, cut into ½-inch pieces

❶ In small bowl, whisk together vinegar and mustard. Slowly whisk in oil. Whisk in tarragon, salt and pepper.

❷ Place beets in another small bowl; toss with generous tablespoon of vinaigrette. Place apple in separate small bowl; toss with another generous tablespoon of vinaigrette. Place salad greens in large bowl and toss with remaining vinaigrette. Divide greens evenly among 6 salad plates. Sprinkle greens evenly with beets, apples and cheese. Serve immediately.

TIP *To cook beets, trim tops to about 2 inches; leave root stem intact. Wash to remove dirt but do not peel until after cooking. Place in medium saucepan with enough water to cover. Add 1 teaspoon salt; boil over medium-high heat until tender, about 20 to 25 minutes for small beets, 35 to 40 for medium and 45 to 50 for large. If cooking a large amount of beets, increase pan size, water volume and salt accordingly.

6 servings.
Preparation time: 20 minutes. Ready to serve: 1 hour, 5 minutes.
Per serving: 270 calories, 23.5 g total fat (6 g saturated fat), 15 mg cholesterol, 125 mg sodium, 2.5 g fiber.

CORN AND BARLEY SALAD

Barley is a grain commonly used in soups and breads, but it makes a delicious addition to this main dish salad.

2/3	cup barley
2	cups cooked corn kernels
1	red bell pepper, cut into 1/2-inch pieces
1/4	cup chopped green onions
1/4	cup extra-virgin olive oil
2	teaspoons grated lime zest
2	tablespoons freshly squeezed lime juice
1	tablespoon chopped fresh cilantro
1/2	teaspoon ground cumin
1/2	teaspoon garlic salt
1/2	teaspoon salt
1/8	teaspoon hot pepper sauce

❶ Cook barley according to package directions. Let cool.

❷ In large bowl, combine barley, corn, bell pepper and onions. In small bowl, whisk together oil, lime zest, lime juice, cilantro, cumin, salts and hot pepper sauce. Pour over barley mixture; toss to coat. Chill several hours to allow flavors to blend.

4 main dish or 6 side dish servings.
Preparation time: 20 minutes. Ready to serve: 3 hours, 30 minutes.

Per main dish serving: 345 calories, 14.5 g total fat (2 g saturated fat), 0 mg cholesterol, 480 mg sodium, 9 g fiber.

FRESH TOMATO SALAD WITH PESTO CROUTONS

Try these tasty croutons in your favorite tomato soup or with other summer salads.

CROUTONS

- 1/4 cup extra-virgin olive oil
- 1/4 cup lightly packed, coarsely chopped fresh basil leaves
- 2 tablespoons freshly grated Parmesan cheese
- 6 (3/4-inch) slices stale baguette, cut into 3/4-inch cubes

DRESSING

- 2 tablespoons extra-virgin olive oil
- 1 tablespoon lemon juice
- 1/4 teaspoon salt
- 1/8 teaspoon freshly ground pepper

SALAD

- 1/4 cup chopped red onion
- 4 cups torn leaf lettuce
- 3 medium red tomatoes, sliced
- 3 medium yellow tomatoes, sliced

❶ Place 1/4 cup oil, basil and cheese in blender or food processor. Pulse to puree. Pour into medium bowl. Add bread; toss to coat. Heat large skillet over medium-high heat until hot. Add bread; cook 5 to 7 minutes or until brown and crispy, turning often. Set aside.

❷ In small bowl whisk together oil, lemon juice, salt and pepper. Set aside.

❸ Place onion in another small bowl; cover with cold water. Soak 15 minutes; drain well. Spread lettuce over serving platter. Top with overlapping rows of tomatoes, alternating colors and beginning with a row of red tomatoes. Repeat until all tomatoes are used. Sprinkle with onion; drizzle with dressing. Sprinkle with croutons.

6 servings.
Preparation time: 15 minutes. Ready to serve: 30 minutes.
Per serving: 200 calories, 15 g total fat (2.5 g saturated fat), 0 mg cholesterol, 235 mg sodium, 2.5 g fiber.

BREAD SALAD WITH GRILLED ZUCCHINI

This popular Italian salad is a great way to use up leftover French bread. Be sure to make it in the summer when tomatoes and basil are at their peak!

1	(8-oz.) slightly stale baguette
3	medium-small (about 3/4 lb.) zucchini, cut lengthwise into 1/2-inch wide strips
1	small red onion, cut into 1/2-inch wide slices
1/2	cup plus 1 tablespoon extra-virgin olive oil
2	large tomatoes, cut into 1-inch pieces
1/2	cup coarsely chopped fresh basil
1/4	cup chopped fresh Italian parsley
1/4	cup red wine vinegar
2	tablespoons water
1 1/2	teaspoons minced garlic
1/2	teaspoon salt
1/4	teaspoon freshly ground pepper
1/4	cup (1 oz.) freshly grated Parmesan cheese

❶ Cut baguette into 1 1/2-inch pieces. Place on tray and allow to dry slightly while preparing remainder of salad.

❷ Heat grill. Brush zucchini and onion slices lightly with 1 tablespoon of the olive oil. Grill zucchini and onion on gas grill over medium heat or on charcoal grill 4 to 6 inches from medium coals 10 minutes, or until crisp tender, turning once. Remove; cool slightly. Cut into 1-inch pieces.

❸ In large bowl, combine bread, zucchini, onion, tomatoes, basil and parsley; toss to combine. In small bowl, whisk together remaining ½ cup oil, vinegar, water, garlic, salt and pepper. Drizzle dressing over salad, tossing to coat. Sprinkle with cheese.

8 servings.
Preparation time: 20 minutes. Ready to serve: 30 minutes.

Per serving: 255 calories, 17.5 g total fat (3 g saturated fat), 5 mg cholesterol, 385 mg sodium, 2.5 g fiber.

ESCAROLE AND FENNEL SALAD WITH ROASTED GARLIC VINAIGRETTE

Ideal in late fall and winter, escarole's bite is complemented by fennel's sweetness. Iceberg lettuce provides a crunchy background, while the roasted garlic vinaigrette pulls everything together.

VINAIGRETTE

- 1 head garlic, roasted*
- 1/3 cup extra-virgin olive oil
- 2 tablespoons red wine vinegar
- 1/2 teaspoon Dijon mustard
- 1/4 teaspoon salt
- 1/8 teaspoon freshly ground pepper

SALAD

- 4 cups bite-size pieces escarole
- 4 cups bite-size pieces iceberg lettuce
- 1 medium fennel bulb, fronds removed, quartered, cut into 1/4-inch slices

❶ In blender, combine roasted garlic, oil, vinegar, mustard, salt and pepper. Puree until creamy and well blended.

❷ Just before serving, toss escarole, lettuce and fennel bulb with vinaigrette.

TIP *To roast garlic, see directions in recipe for *Great Garlicky Dip with Summer Vegetables* (page 29).

6 servings.
Preparation time: 15 minutes. Ready to serve: 1 hour, 15 minutes.

Per serving: 135 calories, 12 g total fat (1.5 g saturated fat), 0 mg cholesterol, 130 mg sodium, 2 g fiber.

OROCCAN CARROT SALAD

Inspired by North African flavors, this salad will quickly become a family favorite.

2   tablespoons lemon juice
1   tablespoon orange juice
1   tablespoon honey
1/2   teaspoon ground cumin
1/2   teaspoon salt
1/4   teaspoon cinnamon
4   large carrots, grated (about 3 cups)

❶ Combine lemon juice, orange juice, honey, cumin, salt and cinnamon in medium bowl; mix well. Add carrots; toss to combine. (Carrots will lose volume when dressed.)

4 servings.
Preparation time: 15 minutes. Ready to serve: 15 minutes.
Per serving: 70 calories, .5 g total fat (0 g saturated fat), 0 mg cholesterol, 330 mg sodium, 3.5 g fiber.

ITALIAN WHEAT BERRY SALAD

Wheat berries are whole kernels of wheat. Look for them in natural food stores. If unavailable, substitute cracked wheat or bulgur, cooked according to package directions.

1	cup wheat berries
2	teaspoons salt
1	yellow bell pepper, cut into 1/2-inch pieces
1	medium carrot, cut into 1/2-inch pieces
12	cherry tomatoes, halved
1	small zucchini, cut into 1/2-inch pieces
1/3	cup chopped fresh basil
1/4	cup finely sliced green onions
1	(6.5-oz.) jar marinated artichoke hearts
6	tablespoons extra-virgin olive oil
3	tablespoons balsamic vinegar
1	teaspoon finely minced garlic
1 1/2	teaspoons chopped fresh rosemary or 1/2 teaspoon dried rosemary, crushed
1/8	teaspoon freshly ground pepper

❶ Place wheat berries in medium saucepan with enough water to cover by several inches. Cook over low heat 2 hours or until tender, adding 1 1/2 teaspoons of the salt during last 30 minutes of cooking. Drain; cool.

❷ In large bowl, combine wheat berries with bell pepper, carrot, tomatoes, zucchini, basil and onions. Drain artichokes, reserving marinade. Cut artichokes into 1/2-inch pieces; add to wheat berry mixture.

❸ In small bowl, combine reserved marinade, oil, vinegar, garlic, rosemary, salt and pepper; mix well. Toss with wheat berry mixture. Chill several hours to allow flavors to blend.

4 main course or 6 side dish servings.
Preparation time: 15 minutes. Ready to serve: 5 hours, 15 minutes.

Per main course serving: 350 calories, 22.5 g total fat (3 g saturated fat), 0 mg cholesterol, 740 mg sodium, 8 g fiber.

GAZPACHO SALAD WITH SPICED CORN CROUTONS

Use leftover cornbread to make these tasty croutons, or feel free to substitute your favorite purchased croutons if time is of the essence.

CROUTONS
- 1½ cups cubed (¾ inch) stale cornbread
- ½ teaspoon chili powder
- ¼ teaspoon garlic salt
- Dash cayenne

SALAD
- 1 large tomato
- 1 medium cucumber, peeled
- 1 small to medium green bell pepper, seeded
- 3 green onions
- 6 cups torn leaf lettuce

DRESSING
- 5 tablespoons extra-virgin olive oil
- 1 tablespoon sherry vinegar or red wine vinegar
- 1 teaspoon minced garlic
- ⅛ teaspoon salt
- Dash cayenne

1. Heat oven to 350°F. Place cornbread in shallow baking pan; spray with nonstick cooking spray. In small bowl, combine chili powder, garlic salt and cayenne; sprinkle over cornbread. Bake 10 minutes or until crisp and browned; let cool.

2. Meanwhile, dice tomato, cucumber and bell pepper. Thinly slice onion. Reserve ¼ cup of the tomato, 2 tablespoons each of the cucumber and bell pepper, and 1 tablespoon of the onion for dressing. Place torn leaf lettuce in medium bowl.

3. In blender combine reserved tomato, cucumber, bell pepper, onion, olive oil, vinegar, garlic, salt and cayenne. Puree until well blended; strain. Reserve ¼ cup of the dressing. Toss lettuce with remaining dressing; divide evenly among 6 salad plates. Sprinkle remaining tomato, cucumber, bell pepper and onion evenly over lettuce; drizzle with reserved dressing. Top with croutons.

6 servings.
Preparation time: 25 minutes. Ready to serve: 25 minutes.

Per serving: 185 calories, 14 g total fat (2.5 g saturated fat), 15 mg cholesterol, 270 mg sodium, 2.5 g fiber.

# WINTER SALAD WITH ENDIVE AND CELERY ROOT

Belgian endive and celery root are both popular ingredients in Parisian salads. To prepare ahead, make vinaigrette and assemble lettuce, endive and celery root. To keep the celery root from darkening, toss with enough vinaigrette to coat. Refrigerate vinaigrette, lettuce, endive and celery root. Toss to combine just before serving.

VINAIGRETTE
- 2 tablespoons Dijon mustard
- 3 tablespoons white wine vinegar
- 2/3 cup vegetable oil
- 1/4 teaspoon salt
- 1/8 teaspoon freshly ground pepper

SALAD
- 4 cups mixed leaf lettuce
- 1 head Belgian endive, cut into 1/2-inch slices
- 1 cup diced celery root

❶ In small bowl, whisk together mustard and vinegar. Slowly whisk in oil; season with salt and pepper.

❷ In large bowl, combine lettuce, endive and celery root. Toss with vinaigrette to coat.

4 to 6 servings.
Preparation time: 20 minutes. Ready to serve: 20 minutes.
Per 4 servings: 360 calories, 37 g total fat (5.5 g saturated fat), 0 mg cholesterol, 280 mg sodium, 5 g fiber.

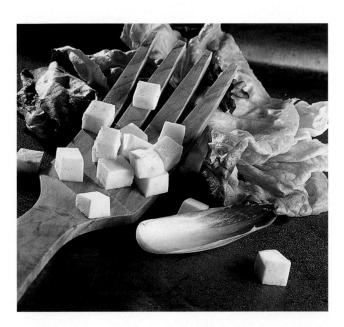

SPICY PEA POD AND ORANGE SALAD

In the early spring, substitute several handfuls of pea shoots from the market for the pea pods. Tahini is a ground sesame paste. If you have trouble finding it, use peanut butter instead.

VINAIGRETTE

- 2 tablespoons cider vinegar
- 1 tablespoon tahini
- 1 teaspoon honey
- 1/2 teaspoon hot pepper sauce
- 1/4 teaspoon salt
- 1/3 cup vegetable oil

SALAD

- 1/2 lb. pea pods
- 6 cups mixed organic greens
- 2 oranges or tangerines, peeled, divided into segments

1. In small bowl, whisk together vinegar, tahini, honey, hot pepper sauce and salt. Slowly whisk in oil.

2. Bring a large saucepan half-filled with water to a boil over high heat. Add pea pods; cook 30 to 60 seconds or until pea pods turn a vivid green. Drain; run under cold water to stop cooking; pat dry. Place greens in large bowl; toss with dressing. Top with pea pods and orange segments. Serve immediately.

6 servings.
Preparation time: 10 minutes. Ready to serve: 10 minutes.

Per serving: 165 calories, 13.5 g total fat (2 g saturated fat), 0 mg cholesterol, 105 mg sodium, 3 g fiber.

SOUPS

The soup pot is an ideal destination for vegetables. Their inherent moisture and intense flavors make them natural additions. Start with some broth or stock and see what the refrigerator has to offer. Throw in some pasta, canned beans or cream to make the finished product even more satisfying. Before you know it, people will be asking you for the recipe.

Borscht with Double Caraway Cream, page 58
Carrot, Orange and Ginger Soup, page 59

BORSCHT WITH DOUBLE CARAWAY CREAM

Charnuska is a small, black seed used in Indian cooking. Also known as black caraway, it is used to top Jewish rye.

CREAM
- 1/2 cup sour cream
- 1/2 teaspoon caraway seeds, lightly crushed
- 1/4 teaspoon charnuska, if desired

BORSCHT
- 2 tablespoons vegetable oil
- 1 large onion, chopped
- 1 teaspoon minced garlic
- 1/2 medium cabbage, shredded
- 2 medium beets, shredded
- 6 cups beef broth or *Rich Vegetable Stock* (page 61)
- 1 (14.5-oz.) can diced tomatoes, undrained
- 3 tablespoons red wine vinegar
- 1/2 teaspoon freshly ground pepper
- 1/2 teaspoon celery salt
- 1 medium potato, cut into 1/2-inch pieces

❶ In small bowl, combine sour cream, caraway and charnuska. Let sit overnight for all flavors to blend.*

❷ Heat oil in nonreactive Dutch oven over medium heat until hot. Add onion; sauté 4 to 5 minutes or until softened. Add garlic; sauté an additional minute or until fragrant. Add cabbage, beets, broth, tomatoes, vinegar, pepper and celery salt. Bring to a boil; reduce heat to low. Simmer, covered, 1 1/2 hours. Add potato during last 45 minutes of cooking. Serve with Double Caraway Cream.

TIP *If unable to do in advance, combine caraway seeds with 2 teaspoons of very hot water; let sit while preparing remainder of recipe. Combine with sour cream and charnuska before serving.

6 main course or 8 first course servings.
Preparation time: 25 minutes. Ready to serve: 8 hours, 25 minutes.

Per main course serving: 180 calories, 9 g total fat (3 g saturated fat), 15 mg cholesterol, 1315 mg sodium, 4 g fiber.

CARROT, ORANGE AND GINGER SOUP

Perfect on a hot summer day, this cold soup bursts with flavor. The acidity of the orange plays against the sweetness of the carrots and the spicy sharpness of the ginger.

5   cups *Light Vegetable Stock* (page 60) or 5 cups water
1   lb. carrots, peeled, cut into 1-inch pieces
2   teaspoons grated fresh ginger
1/4 cup thawed orange juice concentrate
1   teaspoon salt
1/8 teaspoon freshly ground pepper

1 In Dutch oven, bring stock, carrots and ginger to a boil over medium-high heat. Reduce heat to low; simmer, partially covered, 40 to 45 minutes or until carrots are very tender. Remove from heat; cool slightly. Puree carrots and cooking liquid in blender or food processor. Stir in orange juice concentrate, salt and pepper. Chill 3 to 4 hours or overnight.

4 servings.
Preparation time: 15 minutes. Ready to serve: 4 hours.
Per serving: 90 calories, .5 g total fat (0 g saturated fat), 0 mg cholesterol, 620 mg sodium, 3.5 g fiber.

LIGHT VEGETABLE STOCK

This light stock adds flavor to soups and dishes where chicken broth would normally be used. When substituting for canned broth, add 1/4 to 1/2 teaspoon of salt for every cup used.

1	large onion, peeled, halved
2	large carrots, cut into large pieces
1	rib celery, cut into large pieces
1	medium potato, halved
1	bunch green onions
6	stems parsley
1	bay leaf
2	sprigs fresh thyme or 1/2 teaspoon dried
3 to 4	peppercorns
9	cups water

❶ Place all ingredients in Dutch oven. Bring to a boil over medium-high heat. Reduce heat to low; barely simmer, partially covered, 2 hours. Strain. Refrigerate up to 3 days or freeze.

6 cups.
Preparation time: 10 minutes. Ready to serve: 2 hours, 10 minutes.
Per cup: 10 calories, 0 g total fat (0 g saturated fat), 0 mg cholesterol, 5 mg sodium, 0 g fiber.

RICH VEGETABLE STOCK

This homemade stock adds richness and color. Use it as a substitute for beef stocks and broths in recipes. As with the light vegetable stock, if substituting for canned broth, add 1/4 to 1/2 teaspoon of salt for every cup used.

1	large onion, cut in quarters, outer skin removed
1	medium tomato, halved
1	rib celery, cut into large pieces
1	large carrot, cut into large pieces
1	medium potato, halved
1	bunch green onions
1	tablespoon vegetable oil
9	cups water
6	parsley stems
2	sprigs fresh thyme or 1/2 teaspoon dried
3 to 4	peppercorns
1	bay leaf
2	tablespoons soy sauce

1 Heat oven to 400°F. Place onion, tomato, celery, carrot, potato and green onions in large shallow roasting or baking pan. Drizzle with oil; toss to coat. Bake 30 to 40 minutes or until browned, turning every 10 minutes to prevent burning. Remove vegetables; place in large pot.

2 Add 1 cup water to roasting pan. Cook on low heat, scraping up any brown bits from bottom of pan. Pour mixture into large pot.

3 To vegetable mixture, add parsley, thyme, peppercorns, bay leaf, remaining 8 cups water and soy sauce. Bring to a boil over medium-high heat. Reduce heat to low; simmer, partially covered, 2 hours. Strain; refrigerate up to 3 days or freeze.

6 cups.
Preparation time: 10 minutes. Ready to serve: 2 hours, 40 minutes.
Per cup: 40 calories, 2.5 g total fat (.5 g saturated fat), 0 mg cholesterol, 350 mg sodium, .5 g fiber.

CREAMY THREE-POTATO SOUP

Soups can be creamy without a lot of added fat. The pureed potatoes give this soup a rich, velvety texture accented by the subtle flavor of leeks. To clean leeks, trim off root ends and cut the stalks in half lengthwise. Separate sections under running water to remove grit.

2 tablespoons vegetable oil
2 medium leeks, chopped, white and light green portions only
1 medium onion, sliced
6 cups reduced-sodium chicken broth (or 6 cups *Light Vegetable Stock* (page 60) plus 1¼ teaspoons salt)
½ lb. russet potatoes, peeled, sliced
½ lb. Yukon Gold potatoes, peeled, sliced
1 lb. sweet potatoes or yams, peeled, sliced
½ cup milk
¼ teaspoon white pepper

❶ Heat oil in Dutch oven over medium heat until hot. Sauté leeks and onion 3 to 4 minutes. Add broth and potatoes; bring to a boil. Reduce heat to low; simmer, partially covered, about 30 to 40 minutes, or until tender. Remove from heat; cool slightly. Puree in blender or food processor; return to Dutch oven. Stir in milk and pepper. Heat gently over low heat just until hot.

6 main course or 8 first course servings.
Preparation time: 25 minutes. Ready to serve: 1 hour.

Per main course serving: 225 calories, 6.5 g total fat (1.5 g saturated fat), 0 mg cholesterol, 505 mg sodium, 4 g fiber.

CHEDDAR AND VEGETABLE SOUP

This variation on beer cheese soup is hearty and comforting. Make sure to include some of the broccoli stems as well as the buds. Peel the stems before using if the outer skin is tough.

1/4   cup butter
  1   medium onion, chopped (about 1 cup)
  1   rib celery, chopped (about 1/2 cup)
1/2   cup all-purpose flour
  1   (14.5-oz) can reduced-sodium chicken broth
        (or 2 cups *Light Vegetable Stock* (page 60) plus 1/2 teaspoon salt)
  2   cups milk
  1   medium potato, diced
  3   cups chopped broccoli
  1   cup beer
  8   oz. grated extra-sharp cheddar cheese (about 2 cups)
  1   teaspoon Worcestershire sauce
1/2   teaspoon salt
1/8   teaspoon hot pepper sauce

❶ Melt butter in Dutch oven over medium heat. Add onion and celery; sauté 4 to 5 minutes or until softened. Stir in flour. Whisk in broth and milk. Add potato; slowly bring to a boil, stirring occasionally. Reduce heat to low; simmer, partially covered, 10 minutes, stirring occasionally. Stir in broccoli and beer; continue cooking partially covered an additional 15 minutes, stirring occasionally. Stir in cheese, Worcestershire sauce, salt and hot pepper sauce. Serve hot.

6 servings.
Preparation time: 20 minutes. Ready to serve: 45 minutes.

Per serving: 360 calories, 22.5 g total fat (14 g saturated fat), 65 mg cholesterol, 695 mg sodium, 2.5 g fiber.

HERBED LENTIL SOUP

Serve this soup on a cold winter day. Use canned tomatoes for ease of preparation. If you want to use fresh tomatoes, all the better; the tip at the end of this recipe tells you what to substitute.

2 tablespoons olive oil
2 medium onions, chopped (about 2 cups)
2 large carrots, chopped (about 1 cup)
3/4 teaspoon dried thyme
1/2 teaspoon dried oregano
4 cups reduced-sodium chicken broth (or 4 cups
  Light Vegetable Stock (page 60) plus 1 teaspoon salt)
1/2 cup dry red wine
1 cup lentils, rinsed
1 (14.5-oz.) can diced tomatoes, undrained*
2 tablespoons chopped fresh parsley

❶ Heat oil in nonreactive Dutch oven over medium heat until hot. Add onions and carrots; sauté 4 to 5 minutes. Add thyme and oregano; sauté an additional minute. Add broth, wine, lentils and tomatoes. Bring to a boil; reduce heat to low. Simmer, partially covered, 40 to 45 minutes or until lentils are tender. Garnish with fresh chopped parsley.

TIP *One pound chopped, peeled tomatoes plus 1/2 teaspoon salt may be substituted for the canned tomatoes.

6 main course servings.
Preparation time: 15 minutes. Ready to serve: 55 minutes.
Per serving: 220 calories, 6 g total fat (1 g saturated fat), 0 mg cholesterol, 450 mg sodium, 10 g fiber.

SAVORY TOMATO AND GARBANZO BEAN SOUP

A fabulous soup served poolside at the Steltzner Vineyards in the Napa Valley inspired this recipe.

2 tablespoons olive oil
1 large onion, chopped
6 large basil leaves
4 large sage leaves
4 sprigs Italian parsley
   Leaves from 2-inch sprig rosemary
2 large garlic cloves, minced
1 (15-oz.) can garbanzo beans, drained, rinsed
5 medium tomatoes, chopped, juice reserved
1 (14.5-oz.) can reduced-sodium chicken broth (or 2 cups
   Light Vegetable Stock (page 60) plus 1/2 teaspoon salt)
1/8 teaspoon freshly ground pepper

❶ Heat oil in nonreactive Dutch oven over medium heat until hot. Add onion; sauté about 5 minutes, stirring often.

❷ Meanwhile, chop basil, sage, parsley and rosemary together. When onion is softened, add herbs, garlic and beans. Sauté an additional 2 to 3 minutes. Remove half of bean mixture from Dutch oven; reserve.

❸ To Dutch oven, add tomatoes and their juice, broth and pepper; bring to a boil. Reduce heat to medium-low; cook an additional 15 minutes. Remove from heat; puree in blender or food processor. Return to Dutch oven; stir in reserved bean mixture. Bring to a simmer over medium heat.

4 main course or 6 first course servings.
Preparation time: 30 minutes. Ready to serve: 50 minutes.

Per main course serving: 245 calories, 10 g total fat (1.5 g saturated fat), 0 mg cholesterol, 410 mg sodium, 6.5 g fiber.

SPRING ASPARAGUS SOUP

If you are a frugal cook, save the woody ends trimmed from asparagus in other recipes and use them as part of the asparagus called for here. Crème fraîche is a thick, rich, nutty cream available in gourmet supermarkets. Substitute sour cream if unavailable, but do not allow it to boil.

- 1   tablespoon butter
- ¼   cup chopped shallots
- 2   lb. asparagus
- 4   cups reduced-sodium chicken broth (or 4 cups *Light Vegetable Stock* (page 60) plus 1 teaspoon salt)
- ¼   cup plus 2 tablespoons crème fraîche
- 6   spinach leaves, cut into ribbons

❶ In Dutch oven, melt butter over medium heat. Add shallots; sauté 3 to 4 minutes or until softened. Remove tips from asparagus; reserve. Cut spears into 2-inch pieces; add to Dutch oven. Add broth; bring to a boil. Reduce heat to low; simmer 10 minutes or until spears are tender.

❷ Remove asparagus mixture from heat; puree in blender. Strain; return to Dutch oven. Add ¼ cup of the crème fraîche and asparagus tips; simmer 3 to 5 minutes or until asparagus is crisp-tender. If using sour cream, heat through but do not boil. Ladle into bowls; top each bowl with 1 teaspoon of the crème fraîche and 1 spinach leaf.

6 servings.
Preparation time: 20 minutes. Ready to serve: 35 minutes.
Per serving: 110 calories, 8 g total fat (4.5 g saturated fat), 20 mg cholesterol, 350 mg sodium, 1.5 g fiber.

ONION SOUP

Don't be tempted to hurry the onions. They give the soup its distinctive flavor.

    3   tablespoons vegetable oil
    4   large onions, thinly sliced (about 8 cups)
 1¹/₂   teaspoons sugar
  ¹/₄   teaspoon salt
  ¹/₈   teaspoon pepper
    5   cups beef broth plus 1 cup water (or 3 cups *Rich Vegetable Stock* (page 61) plus 1 teaspoon salt)
  ¹/₂   cup dry white wine
6 to 8 slices stale baguette (1 inch thick), toasted
 1¹/₂   cups (6 oz.) shredded Gruyère or Emmentaler cheese

❶ Heat oil in nonreactive Dutch oven over medium-high heat until hot. Add onions; stir to coat. Sauté 5 to 7 minutes until onions begin to soften, turning occasionally. Reduce heat to low; sprinkle with sugar; cover and cook 30 minutes, stirring occasionally. Uncover; increase heat to medium. Continue cooking 20 to 25 minutes or until onions turn a rich brown. (As onions begin to brown, scrape bottom of pan with a wooden spoon to incorporate caramel color into onions and to prevent scorching.) Stir in broth and wine; bring to a boil. Reduce heat to low; simmer, partially covered, 30 minutes. Season with salt and pepper, if desired.

❷ Heat broiler; ladle hot soup into oven-proof bowls. Top with 1 slice bread for first course serving or 2 for main course; sprinkle with cheese. Place bowls on baking sheet; broil until cheese is melted.

4 main course or 6 first course servings.
Preparation time: 40 minutes. Ready to serve: 1 hour, 45 minutes.

Per main course serving: 415 calories, 23 g total fat (9.5 g saturated fat), 40 mg cholesterol, 1690 mg sodium, 3.5 g fiber.

WILD RICE AND MUSHROOM SOUP

Wild rice is not really a rice but rather a marsh grass. It adds a wonderful, nutty flavor to this soup. Pancetta is a cured, unsmoked Italian bacon. If unavailable, substitute regular bacon, simmering it in water for 10 minutes to remove the smoky flavor. Drain and thoroughly pat dry before using. Vegetarians can omit the pancetta and increase the oil to three tablespoons.

- 1 (1-oz.) pkg. dried wild mushrooms
- 1 cup very hot water (115°F to 120°F)
- 1 tablespoon vegetable oil
- 1 cup diced pancetta
- 1/4 cup chopped shallots or green onions
- 1 (8-oz.) pkg. mushrooms, sliced
- 1/3 cup all-purpose flour
- 2 cups milk
- 1 (14.5-oz.) can chicken broth (or an additional 2 cups milk plus 3/4 teaspoon salt)
- 2 cups cooked wild rice*

❶ Soak dried mushrooms in very hot water in medium bowl 30 minutes. Remove mushrooms; chop. Strain soaking liquid through coffee filter to remove grit; set aside.

❷ Heat oil in Dutch oven over medium-high heat until hot. Add pancetta; sauté 1 minute. Add shallots; sauté 3 to 5 minutes or until tender and pancetta is browned. Add mushrooms; sauté 5 to 8 minutes or until tender. Add chopped wild mushrooms and reserved soaking liquid. Cook 5 minutes or until all liquid is absorbed. Stir in flour; whisk in milk and broth. Bring to a boil; continue cooking, stirring, for several minutes to thicken. Stir in rice; reduce heat to low. Simmer 5 minutes.

TIP *To cook wild rice, rinse ¾ cup wild rice under cold water. Place in medium saucepan with 2½ cups water. Add ¾ teaspoon salt. Bring to a boil over medium-high heat. Reduce heat to low; cover and cook 45 to 60 minutes or until grains have opened and rice is chewy-tender. Drain if necessary.

4 main course or 6 first course servings.
Preparation time: 30 minutes. Ready to serve: 1 hour, 20 minutes.

Per main course serving: 295 calories, 11 g total fat (3.5 g saturated fat), 15 mg cholesterol, 905 mg sodium, 3 g fiber.

WINTER SOUP AU PISTOU

Pistou is the French equivalent of pesto. Make pistou (or pesto) in the summertime when fresh basil is abundant; freeze in small amounts to savor during the colder months.

2	tablespoons extra-virgin olive oil
1	medium onion, chopped
1½	teaspoons minced garlic
1	cup cubed peeled butternut squash
1	green bell pepper, diced
1	rib celery, chopped
1	medium carrot, chopped
1	small potato, cubed
6	cups *Light Vegetable Stock* (page 60)
1	(14.5-oz.) can diced tomatoes, undrained
1	(15-oz.) can cannellini beans, drained, rinsed
½	cup broken vermicelli or capellini
¾	teaspoon salt
¼	teaspoon freshly ground pepper

PISTOU

1	cup packed fresh basil
½	cup fresh parsley, leaves only
1	teaspoon chopped garlic
¼	cup (1 oz.) freshly grated Parmesan cheese
¼	cup extra-virgin olive oil

❶ Heat 2 tablespoons oil in nonreactive Dutch oven over medium heat until hot. Add onion; sauté 4 to 5 minutes or until softened. Add 1½ teaspoons garlic; sauté 1 minute or until fragrant. Add squash, bell pepper, celery, carrot and potato; stir to combine. Add stock and tomatoes; stir to combine. Bring to a boil; reduce heat to low. Simmer, partially covered, 20 minutes. Add beans, vermicelli, salt and pepper. Simmer an additional 5 minutes.

❷ In food processor, combine basil, parsley and 1 teaspoon garlic; pulse to combine. Add cheese; pulse several times. With motor running, slowly pour in ¼ cup olive oil. To serve, spoon 1 tablespoon pistou into center of each bowl of soup. Pass extra in small bowl.

8 servings.
Preparation time: 45 minutes. Ready to serve: 1 hour, 10 minutes.
Per serving: 230 calories, 12 g total fat (2 g saturated fat), 5 mg cholesterol, 655 mg sodium, 5.5 g fiber.

SIDES

Sometimes the sidekick should be the star. In terms of interest, the supporting role is sometimes the strongest. So it is with vegetable side dishes. Often downplayed, they can instead become the highlight of a meal. A simple main dish becomes a winner when paired with a flavorful side. Use these recipes and the tips in the Technique & Tools section to serve up the following scene (or plate) stealers.

Caribbean Carrots with Lime Butter, page 76

CARIBBEAN CARROTS WITH LIME BUTTER

Allspice, sometimes referred to as Jamaican pepper, is the berry of the evergreen tree. Along with the lime and hot sauce, the allspice gives a characteristic Caribbean flavor.

1/4 cup water
2 tablespoons sugar
2 teaspoons grated lime peel
1/2 teaspoon ground allspice
1/4 teaspoon ground nutmeg
1/4 teaspoon salt
1/8 teaspoon hot pepper sauce
1 (1-lb.) pkg. baby carrots or 2 lbs. fresh carrots, trimmed
2 tablespoons butter

1 In medium saucepan, bring water, sugar, 1 teaspoon of the lime peel, allspice, nutmeg, salt and hot pepper sauce to a boil over medium heat. Add carrots; stir to coat. Reduce heat to low; cover and cook 8 to 10 minutes or until carrots are almost tender.

2 Uncover; increase heat to high. Cook until cooking liquid evaporates, stirring often. Remove from heat; toss with butter and remaining 1 teaspoon lime peel.

6 servings.
Preparation time: 10 minutes. Ready to serve: 18 minutes.
Per serving: 85 calories, 4 g total fat (2.5 g saturated fat), 10 mg cholesterol, 150 mg sodium, 2.5 g fiber.

CONFETTI RISOTTO

Serve this colorful risotto as a side dish or on its own as a main course.

   5 cups water
   1 large carrot, cut into 1/2-inch pieces (about 1/2 cup)
 1/2 red bell pepper, cut into 1/2-inch pieces (about 1/2 cup)
 1/2 medium yellow squash, cut into 1/2-inch pieces (about 1/2 cup)
 1/2 cup shelled peas
 1/2 cup white wine
   1 tablespoon soy sauce
 1/8 teaspoon salt
   2 tablespoons butter
   1 small onion, chopped
1 1/2 cups arborio rice
 1/2 cup (2 oz.) freshly grated Parmesan cheese

❶ Bring water to a boil in medium saucepan over medium-high heat. Add carrot; cook 5 minutes. Add bell pepper, squash and peas; cook an additional 5 minutes. Drain vegetables, reserving water. Set aside vegetables; return water to saucepan. Add wine, soy sauce and salt. Reduce heat to low; cover and keep wine mixture simmering while making risotto.

❷ Melt butter in large heavy saucepan over medium heat. Add onion; cook 4 to 5 minutes or until tender. Stir in rice; cook 2 to 3 minutes. Reduce heat to medium-low; add 1 cup wine mixture. Cook until liquid is absorbed, stirring often. Continue to add wine mixture 1 cup at a time, cooking and stirring often until rice is just slightly resistant to the bite and creamy, about 30 minutes. Stir in reserved vegetables and cheese.

6 side dish or 4 main dish servings.
Preparation time: 50 minutes. Ready to serve: 1 hour.

Per side dish serving: 280 calories, 7 g total fat (4.5 g saturated fat), 20 mg cholesterol, 440 mg sodium, 2.5 g fiber.

CORN RELISH

Bring this tasty relish to your next summer potluck. It's great with brats and hamburgers. For more elegant fare, try it with grilled salmon.

1/2 cup water
1/2 cup cider vinegar
1/3 cup sugar
3 cups corn (about 6 medium ears)
1 red bell pepper, chopped
1 small onion, halved, thinly sliced
1 Anaheim or New Mexico chile, seeded, chopped
2 teaspoons salt
1 teaspoon mustard seeds
1/2 teaspoon celery seeds
1/2 teaspoon ground turmeric
1/4 teaspoon hot pepper sauce
4 teaspoons all-purpose flour

❶ Bring all ingredients except 1/4 cup of the water and flour to a boil in large saucepan over medium-high heat. Reduce heat to low; simmer 5 minutes. In small bowl, whisk flour into remaining 1/4 cup water; stir into relish. Cook an additional 2 minutes to thicken. Spoon into clean jars. Store in refrigerator up to 2 weeks.

4 cups.
Preparation time: 15 minutes. Ready to serve: 22 minutes.

Per cup: 200 calories, 1 g total fat (0 g saturated fat), 0 mg cholesterol, 1175 mg sodium, 4 g fiber.

BRAISED BEANS IN HOISIN SAUCE

Hoisin sauce is a flavorful ingredient common to Asian cooking. Look for it in your supermarket or in Asian grocery stores.

1   tablespoon vegetable oil
2   teaspoons minced garlic
2   teaspoons minced fresh ginger
1   lb. green beans, trimmed
1/2 cup water
1/4 cup hoisin sauce

❶ Heat oil in large nonstick skillet over medium-high heat until hot. Add garlic and ginger; sauté 30 to 60 seconds or until fragrant. Immediately add green beans; toss to coat.

❷ Combine water and hoisin sauce in small bowl. Pour over beans. Reduce heat to low; cover and cook 20 to 25 minutes, or until beans are tender and sauce has thickened enough to coat beans, stirring occasionally. If beans finish cooking before sauce has thickened, remove them from the skillet; place on large bowl. Increase heat to high; reduce sauce slightly to thicken. Pour sauce over beans.

4 servings.
Preparation time: 15 minutes. Ready to serve: 35 minutes.
Per serving: 90 calories, 4.5 g total fat (.5 g saturated fat), 0 mg cholesterol, 10 mg sodium, 3.5 g fiber.

GARLIC SCALLOPED POTATOES WITH PARMESAN CRUMB CRUST

Cooking the freshly sliced potatoes with the milk thickens the mixture before baking it in the oven. Garlic gives the distinctive flavor and the crumbs add a nice crunch. Make your own bread crumbs by drying leftover bread. Pulse the bread in a food processor fitted with a metal blade to make fine crumbs.

1¾ cups milk
1 tablespoon chopped garlic
½ teaspoon salt
⅛ teaspoon freshly ground pepper
2 lb. Yukon Gold potatoes, peeled if desired, sliced ⅛ inch thick (about 6 cups)
⅓ cup dry bread crumbs
¼ cup (1 oz.) freshly grated Parmesan cheese
1 tablespoon olive oil

❶ Heat oven to 375°F. Spray 8 x 12-inch (or 9 x 13-inch) baking dish with nonstick cooking spray. Heat milk, garlic, salt and pepper in Dutch oven over medium-low heat. Add potatoes; stir to coat. Bring to a simmer, stirring gently. Cook 2 to 3 minutes or until milk begins to thicken. Pour into baking dish. Bake 50 minutes or until potatoes are bubbling.

❷ In small bowl, combine bread crumbs and cheese. Add oil; toss to coat. Sprinkle bread crumb mixture over potatoes. Return to oven; cook an additional 15 to 20 minutes or until crumbs are browned and potatoes are tender.

6 servings.
Preparation time: 20 minutes. Ready to serve: 1 hour, 25 minutes.
Per serving: 235 calories, 5.5 g total fat (2 g saturated fat), 10 mg cholesterol, 380 mg sodium, 3 g fiber.

GREEN BEANS PROVENCALE

Herbes de Provence is a blend of dried spices common to the southern France area called Provence. The blend can vary in content, but usually contains thyme, savory, marjoram, basil and sometimes lavender. This dish can easily be doubled to serve a larger crowd; use a wok instead of a skillet to rewarm the beans.

> 2 lb. green beans, trimmed
> 2 tablespoons olive oil
> 1 red bell pepper, cut into strips
> 1½ teaspoons herbes de Provence
> ¼ teaspoon salt
> ¼ cup pine nuts, toasted, if desired

❶ Bring 2 quarts water to a boil in large pot over high heat. Add beans; return to a boil. Cook beans until crisp-tender, about 10 minutes. Drain; run under cold water to stop cooking. (Beans may be cooked ahead. Cover and refrigerate.)

❷ Heat oil in large skillet over medium-high heat until hot. Add bell pepper; sauté 1 to 2 minutes. Add beans; cook 5 minutes or until heated, stirring occasionally. Sprinkle with herbes de Provence and salt; stir to coat. Serve topped with pine nuts.

8 servings.
Preparation time: 20 minutes. Ready to serve: 35 minutes.

Per serving: 80 calories, 6 g total fat (1 g saturated fat), 0 mg cholesterol, 85 mg sodium, 3.5 g fiber.

CHIPOTLE MASHED POTATOES

The buttery color of Yukon Gold potatoes make them seem extra rich. Serve with grilled chicken, fish or roast pork. For a vegetarian entrée, top with colorful stir-fried peppers and onions.

2   lb. Yukon Gold potatoes (3 to 4 medium), peeled, quartered
1   teaspoon salt
1   large garlic clove, peeled
1   chipotle pepper in adobo sauce, drained, finely minced
1/2   cup hot half-and-half or milk
2   tablespoons butter
1/2   teaspoon salt
1/8   teaspoon freshly ground pepper

❶ Place potatoes in large saucepan; add water to cover. Add salt and garlic; cook over medium heat 25 to 30 minutes or until potatoes are very tender. Drain; return potatoes and garlic to pan. Add pepper. Mash mixture until potatoes are fluffy and have no lumps. Stir in hot half-and-half and butter. Season with salt and pepper.

6 servings.
Preparation time: 15 minutes. Ready to serve: 40 minutes.
Per serving: 180 calories, 6.5 g total fat (4 g saturated fat), 20 mg cholesterol, 640 mg sodium, 2.5 g fiber.

POTATO PANCAKES WITH ROSEMARY

Blanching the potatoes before frying gives them a perfect texture. Serve these pancakes with a dollop of sour cream or applesauce, if desired.

2   medium russet potatoes (about 3/4 lb.)
2   eggs, lightly beaten
1   tablespoon minced garlic
2   teaspoons minced fresh rosemary or 3/4 teaspoon dried
1/4   teaspoon salt
1/8   teaspoon freshly ground pepper
3   tablespoons oil

❶ Bring 2 quarts water to a boil in large pot over high heat. In food processor, shred potatoes to make 2 cups. Immediately drop potatoes into water; cook 1 minute. Strain; run under cold water to stop cooking. Place in towel; squeeze to remove excess moisture. Place in medium bowl; add eggs, garlic, rosemary, salt and pepper. Mix well.

❷ Heat 2 tablespoons of the oil in large skillet over medium-high heat until hot. Drop potato mixture by large mounded spoonfuls into skillet; flatten slightly to form 3-inch pancakes. Cook 7 to 9 minutes or until browned on both sides, turning once. Remove from skillet; set aside. Add remaining 1 tablespoon oil to pan; repeat with remaining potato mixture.

6 servings.
Preparation time: 13 minutes. Ready to serve: 27 minutes.
Per serving: 125 calories, 8.5 g total fat (1.5 g saturated fat), 70 mg cholesterol, 120 mg sodium, 1 g fiber.

RATATOUILLE PEPPERS

Visit your local farmers' market in late summer to find the ingredients you need for this dish. Try serving these peppers with grilled tuna steaks. Turn them into a delicious vegetarian entrée by serving two stuffed pepper halves per person, along with a fresh, tossed salad and French bread.

3 tablespoons olive oil
1 large onion (about ½ lb.), chopped
1 tablespoon minced garlic
½ lb. peeled eggplant, cut into 1-inch pieces (3 cups)
½ lb. zucchini, cut into 1-inch pieces (2 cups)
1 yellow or orange bell pepper (about ½ lb.), cut into 1-inch pieces
2 large tomatoes (about 1 lb.), peeled, cut into 1-inch pieces
¼ cup chopped fresh basil
½ teaspoon salt
¼ teaspoon freshly ground pepper
3 red bell peppers, halved, seeded
3 tablespoons freshly grated Parmesan cheese

❶ Heat oil in nonreactive Dutch oven over medium-high heat until hot. Add onion; sauté 3 to 4 minutes or until softened. Add garlic; sauté an additional minute or until fragrant. Add eggplant, zucchini and yellow bell pepper; sauté an additional 4 to 5 minutes. Add tomatoes, basil, salt and pepper. Reduce heat to low; cook, covered, 15 minutes, stirring occasionally. Uncover; increase heat to medium. Cook about 10 to 15 minutes or until almost all cooking liquid has evaporated. Dish may be made up to 1 day ahead at this point. Cover and refrigerate.

❷ Heat oven to 350°F. Line baking sheet with foil. Place red bell peppers cut side up on baking sheet. Divide ratatouille mixture evenly among peppers. Top with cheese. Bake about 30 minutes or until peppers are crisp-tender and ratatouille is hot.

6 servings.
Preparation time: 40 minutes. Ready to serve: 1 hour, 25 minutes.
Per serving: 130 calories, 8 g total fat (1.5 g saturated fat), 0 mg cholesterol, 260 mg sodium, 3.5 g fiber.

ROASTED PARSNIPS AND ONIONS WITH SAGE

Pair this side dish with roasted turkey or pork.

- 1 lb. parsnips (about 6 medium), peeled, cut in 1/4-inch slices
- 2 medium onions (about 3/4 lb.), sliced 1/2-inch thick
- 2 tablespoons olive oil
- 1 tablespoon honey
- 1 tablespoon balsamic vinegar
- 1 tablespoon finely chopped fresh sage
- 1/4 teaspoon salt
- 1/8 teaspoon freshly ground pepper

❶ Heat oven to 400°F. Combine parsnips and onions in large bowl. In small bowl, stir together oil, honey and vinegar. Pour over vegetables; toss to coat. Spread vegetables on large shallow baking sheet. Bake 40 to 45 minutes, stirring every 15 minutes.

❷ In small bowl, combine sage, salt and pepper. Toss vegetables with seasonings; return to oven. Cook an additional 2 to 3 minutes.

4 servings.
Preparation time: 10 minutes. Ready to serve: 52 minutes.

Per serving: 180 calories, 7 g total fat (1 g saturated fat), 0 mg cholesterol, 155 mg sodium, 5 g fiber.

SPICY MIXED GREENS

Check the glossary to see just how healthy this dish is for you. The crushed red pepper flakes and ginger accent the flavor of the mustard greens, and the tomato adds a bright color note.

2	tablespoons vegetable oil
1	large onion, chopped
1	tablespoon minced fresh ginger
1/2	teaspoon crushed red pepper flakes
1/2	cup reduced-sodium chicken broth or *Light Vegetable Stock* (page 60)
1	bunch collard greens (about 1 lb.), spines removed, cut into large pieces
1/2	bunch kale leaves (about 1/2 lb.), spines removed, cut into large pieces
1	bunch mustard greens (about 1/2 lb.), spines removed, cut into large pieces
1/4	teaspoon salt
1	large tomato, chopped

❶ Heat oil in nonreactive Dutch oven over medium-high heat until hot. Add onion; sauté 5 to 7 minutes or until onion softens and begins to brown. Add ginger and pepper flakes; sauté about 30 seconds. Add broth, collard greens and kale. Reduce heat to medium-low; cover and braise 10 minutes. (If Dutch oven is not large enough to accommodate all the greens at once, add as many as the pan will hold; cover for about one minute. As the greens in the pan shrink during cooking, add more greens until all the collard greens and kale have been added.)

❷ Add mustard greens; braise, covered, an additional 10 minutes. Add salt and tomato; cook, uncovered, an additional 1 to 2 minutes or until tomato is just heated through. With slotted spoon, remove greens and tomato; place in large bowl.

❸ Increase heat to high; reduce remaining cooking juices until lightly syrupy. Toss with greens.

6 servings. Preparation time: 25 minutes. Ready to serve: 50 minutes.

Per serving: 95 calories, 5 g total fat (1 g saturated fat), 0 mg cholesterol, 165 mg sodium, 4 g fiber.

SESAME ASPARAGUS

Make sure you purchase toasted, dark sesame oil for use in this dish. Used as a flavoring agent in this or any other Asian cooking, it adds a rich, nutty flavor.

1 tablespoon oyster sauce
1 tablespoon soy sauce
1 tablespoon dry sherry or white wine
1 teaspoon cornstarch
1½ teaspoons dark sesame oil
2 tablespoons sesame seeds
1 tablespoon vegetable oil
1½ teaspoons minced fresh ginger
1 teaspoon minced garlic
1 lb. asparagus, trimmed, cut diagonally into 1½-inch pieces
1 large carrot, cut diagonally into thin pieces
½ cup chicken broth or water
1 bunch green onions, cut diagonally into 1-inch pieces

1 In small bowl, combine oyster sauce, soy sauce and sherry. Add cornstarch; stir to dissolve. Stir in sesame oil. Set aside.

2 Place sesame seeds in unheated wok. Brown over medium heat until seeds turn golden, about 2 to 3 minutes. Remove seeds; set aside. Increase heat to high. Add oil; swirl to coat wok. Add ginger, garlic, asparagus and carrot. Stir-fry 2 minutes. Add broth; cover and cook an additional 2 minutes or until asparagus and carrot are almost crisp-tender. Uncover. Add green onions. Stir-fry an additional minute. Add oyster sauce mixture; stir until thickened. Toss with sesame seeds.

4 servings.
Preparation time: 30 minutes. Ready to serve: 30 minutes.
Per serving: 125 calories, 8 g total fat (1 g saturated fat), 0 mg cholesterol, 575 mg sodium, 3 g fiber.

PUMPKIN COUSCOUS

Harissa* is a highly seasoned North African condiment available in specialty food shops. It adds extra heat and flavor to couscous and other regional dishes.

1	(10-oz.) pkg. couscous
2	cups *Light Vegetable Stock* (page 60) or water
3	medium tomatoes, chopped
1½	teaspoons ground ginger
½	teaspoon ground nutmeg
½	teaspoon ground allspice
½	teaspoon ground cardamom
½	teaspoon cinnamon
½	teaspoon turmeric
½	teaspoon salt
¼	teaspoon ground coriander
¼	teaspoon freshly ground pepper
¼	teaspoon cayenne
1	(¾-pound) pumpkin, seeded, peeled, cut into 1½-inch chunks
10 to 12	baby carrots
1	medium onion, cut into 1½-inch chunks
1	turnip, cut into 1½-inch chunks
½	cup raisins

❶ Cook couscous according to package directions.

❷ In large saucepan, combine stock, tomatoes, ginger, nutmeg, allspice, cardamom, cinnamon, turmeric, salt, coriander, pepper and cayenne; mix well. Bring to a boil; add pumpkin, carrots, onion, turnip and just enough water to cover. Return to a boil. Reduce heat to simmer about 20 minutes or until vegetables are tender. Stir in raisins.

❸ On platter, make ring with couscous. Place vegetables in center; drizzle with broth. Serve remaining broth mixed with harissa, if desired.

TIP *Hot pepper sauce can be substituted.

4 to 6 servings.
Preparation time: 20 minutes. Ready to serve: 1 hour.
Per serving: 390 calories, 1.5 g total fat (.5 g saturated fat), 0 mg cholesterol, 330 mg sodium, 9 g fiber.

*L*EEK AND BOK CHOY GRATIN

Looking for a change from the ordinary? Simple to prepare, this dish is amazingly good.

1	lb. leeks, white and pale green portions, cut into 1¹/₂-inch pieces (about 4 cups)
1	lb. bok choy, stems and leaves, cut into 1¹/₂-inch pieces (about 5 cups)
¹/₂	cup chicken broth (or ¹/₂ cup water plus 1 tablespoon soy sauce)
1	tablespoon all-purpose flour
1	cup (4 oz.) grated Gruyère or other Swiss-style cheese

❶ Heat oven to 350°F. In large bowl, combine leeks and bok choy; toss. Place in 8 x 12-inch (or 9 x 13-inch) baking dish.

❷ In small bowl, whisk together broth and flour. Pour over leek mixture. Cover tightly with foil; bake 45 minutes, stirring once after 30 minutes. Remove from oven. Stir; sprinkle with cheese. Return to oven, uncovered; bake an additional 10 to 15 minutes or until cheese is melted.

6 servings.
Preparation time: 10 minutes. Ready to serve: 1 hour, 5 minutes.

Per serving: 100 calories, 5.5 g total fat (3.5 g saturated fat), 15 mg cholesterol, 190 mg sodium, 1.5 g fiber.

SPINACH TIMBALES

Timbale refers to the round, high-sided mold that tapers slightly and is used for baking, as well as the dish that is baked in the mold. Timbale molds can be purchased in some specialty cookware stores. Custard cups provide an easier alternative. Using frozen spinach in this recipe speeds the cooking process without sacrificing taste.

TIMBALES
- 1 tablespoon butter
- 1/4 cup minced onion
- 1 1/2 teaspoons minced garlic
- 1 1/2 teaspoons minced fresh ginger
- 1/4 cup tomato sauce
- 1/2 tablespoon coriander
- 1/2 teaspoon cumin
- 1/4 teaspoon ground red pepper
- 1/4 teaspoon salt
- 1/8 teaspoon turmeric
- 1 (10-oz.) pkg. frozen chopped spinach, thawed
- 1/4 cup (1 oz.) freshly grated Parmesan cheese
- 3/4 cup crème fraîche or buttermilk
- 3 eggs

SAUCE
- 1 lb. tomatoes, peeled
- 2 teaspoons finely minced fresh ginger
- 1/4 teaspoon salt

❶ Heat oven to 350°F. Butter 6 (6-oz.) custard cups or timbale molds.

❷ Melt butter in medium skillet over medium heat. Add onion, garlic and ginger; sauté 5 to 8 minutes or until browned. Add tomato sauce, coriander, cumin, red pepper, salt and turmeric. Simmer, covered, about 5 minutes or until a film of oil forms on sauce. Squeeze spinach to remove excess moisture; add to tomato sauce. Simmer, covered, 10 minutes. Remove from heat; cool.

③ In food processor, puree spinach mixture. Add cheese; pulse to combine. Add crème fraîche and eggs; puree until smooth.

④ Divide mixture evenly among custard cups. Place in large shallow pan; add enough boiling water to pan to come halfway up sides of molds. Bake about 30 minutes or until spinach just begins to pull away from edges of molds.

⑤ Meanwhile, puree tomatoes, ginger and salt in food processor to form a slightly chunky sauce. Place in small saucepan; simmer over low heat just until hot.

⑥ Unmold timbales; serve with tomato sauce.

6 servings.
Preparation time: 25 minutes. Ready to serve: 1 hour, 10 minutes.

Per serving: 195 calories, 15.5 g total fat (8.5 g saturated fat), 150 mg cholesterol, 435 mg sodium, 2 g fiber.

RED CABBAGE WITH APPLES AND ALLSPICE

Vinegar helps the red cabbage keep its color while cooking, as well as adding a pleasant tartness.

- 2 tablespoons vegetable oil
- 1 large onion, chopped
- 1 teaspoon minced garlic
- 1 small head red cabbage (about 1½ lb.), shredded
- 1 cup apple cider
- 2 tablespoons apple cider vinegar
- ¾ teaspoon dried thyme
- ¼ teaspoon ground allspice
- 2 medium apples (such as Granny Smith or Golden Delicious), peeled, cut into ½-inch pieces
- ¼ teaspoon salt
- ⅛ teaspoon freshly ground pepper

❶ Heat oil in nonreactive Dutch oven or large pot over medium heat until hot. Add onion and garlic; sauté 4 to 5 minutes or until tender. Add cabbage, apple cider, cider vinegar, thyme and allspice; mix well. Reduce heat to low; cook, covered, 15 minutes, stirring occasionally.

❷ Add apples; cover and cook an additional 10 minutes. Uncover; increase heat to medium. Cook an additional 10 to 15 minutes or until most liquid evaporates, stirring frequently. Season with salt and pepper. (Cabbage should have a slight peppery heat.)

8 servings.
Preparation time: 17 minutes. Ready to serve: 52 minutes.

Per serving: 90 calories, 4 g total fat (.5 g saturated fat), 0 mg cholesterol, 85 mg sodium, 2.5 g fiber.

MAIN DISHES

This chapter has it all — pastas, chilies, sandwiches and brunch dishes, plus exciting flavors from regional American and ethnic cuisines. Some recipes come together quickly; others benefit from slow cooking. Pick one for a busy schedule, another for a lazy afternoon. Meat or no meat, the choice is yours with vegetarian options included for the recipes calling for meat.

Onion Tart, page 100

ONION TART

Similar to a quiche, this flavorful tart makes a wonderful luncheon dish or main course. Serve with Winter Salad with Endive and Celery Root *(page 53) or* Spicy Pea Pod and Orange Salad *(page 55).*

1   (9-inch) pie shell
2   tablespoons vegetable oil
1   tablespoon butter
4   cups thinly sliced onions
3   eggs
1/2   cup heavy cream
3/4   teaspoon salt
1/8   teaspoon freshly ground pepper
1/8   teaspoon caraway seeds
      Dash ground nutmeg
1/2   cup (2 oz.) grated Gruyère or Emmentaler cheese

❶ Heat oven to 400°F. Place crust in a 9-inch tart pan with removable bottom or pie pan. Line crust with foil; fill bottom with pie weights (dried beans or rice can also be used). Bake 12 minutes or until crust is set. Remove foil and weights; return crust to oven. Bake an additional 5 minutes or until crust begins to brown. Remove from oven; cool on wire rack.

❷ Heat oil and butter in large deep pot over medium-high heat until butter is melted. Add onions; sauté 4 to 5 minutes, or until slightly softened, stirring often. Reduce heat to low; cover and cook an additional 20 to 30 minutes, or until onions are very soft, stirring occasionally. Remove; cool slightly.

❸ In large bowl, combine eggs, cream, salt, pepper, caraway seeds and nutmeg; mix well. Stir in onions and 1/4 cup of the cheese. Pour into pie shell. Sprinkle with remaining 1/4 cup cheese. Bake 30 to 35 minutes or until tart is puffy and golden.

4 main dish or 6 luncheon servings.
Preparation time: 20 minutes. Ready to serve: 1 hour.

Per main dish serving: 490 calories, 37 g total fat (15 g saturated fat), 215 mg cholesterol, 755 mg sodium, 2.5 g fiber.

SPAGHETTI SQUASH PUTTANESCA

Pasta puttanesca is a classic Italian dish. Using spaghetti squash instead of the more familiar noodles makes this flavorful entrée even more colorful.

1   (2½- to 3-lb.) spaghetti squash
1   tablespoon olive oil
1   tablespoon minced garlic
2   lb. tomatoes, peeled, cut into 1-inch chunks
1   (2.5-oz.) jar pitted Spanish green olives, drained, coarsely chopped
2   tablespoons capers
¼   teaspoon crushed red pepper flakes
¼   teaspoon salt

❶ Heat oven to 375°F. Place squash in shallow baking pan; prick several times with tip of knife. Bake 1 hour or until outer skin yields when pressed.

❷ Meanwhile, heat oil in large skillet over medium-high heat until hot. Add garlic; sauté 1 to 2 minutes or until fragrant and golden. Add tomatoes; cook 10 minutes. Add olives, capers, red pepper flakes and salt; cook an additional 10 minutes or until mixture thickens.

❸ Remove squash from oven; halve and remove seeds. Using spoon, remove flesh; separate into spaghetti-like strings. Place on large platter. Top with sauce.

4 servings.
Preparation time: 20 minutes. Ready to serve: 1 hour, 15 minutes.

Per serving: 165 calories, 6 g total fat (1 g saturated fat), 0 mg cholesterol, 550 mg sodium, 6 g fiber.

BLACK BEAN, CORN AND BELL PEPPER TART

The cornmeal crust is a take-off on a Mexican tamale filling. To make this colorful dish even spicier, leave the seeds in the jalapeño before chopping.

CRUST
1½ teaspoons chili powder
1 teaspoon baking powder
1 teaspoon cumin
¾ teaspoon salt
2 tablespoons vegetable oil
1¼ cups cornmeal
1 cup boiling water
1 egg

FILLING
1 (15-oz.) can black beans, rinsed, drained
1½ cups cooked corn
1 red bell pepper, diced
½ cup chopped green onions
½ cup coarsely chopped cilantro
1 large jalapeño pepper, seeded, minced
¼ teaspoon salt
⅛ teaspoon freshly ground pepper
1½ cups shredded cheddar and mozzarella cheese blend

GARNISH
1 cup salsa

❶ Heat oven to 400°F. Grease 10-inch springform pan or pie plate with nonstick cooking spray. In medium bowl, combine chili powder, baking powder, cumin and salt; mix well. Stir in oil. Mix in cornmeal until evenly coated. Stir in water; let sit several minutes. Beat in egg. Press cornmeal mixture over bottom and ½ inch up sides of springform pan.

❷ In another medium bowl, combine all filling ingredients except ½ cup of the cheese; mix well. Spoon into crust, pressing down slightly. Sprinkle with remaining ½ cup cheese. Bake 30 minutes or until heated through and cheese is melted. Remove sides of springform pan. Serve with salsa.

6 servings.
Preparation time: 20 minutes. Ready to serve: 50 minutes.
Per serving: 380 calories, 14 g total fat (5.5 g saturated fat), 60 mg cholesterol, 880 mg sodium, 8 g fiber.

BEEF AND PORTOBELLO MUSHROOM POT PIE

Use Rich Vegetable Stock (page 61) for the canned beef broth and add ½ teaspoon salt. The mashed potato crust is outstanding.

FILLING
- 2 tablespoons vegetable oil
- 1 lb. lean beef for stew, cut into ¾-inch cubes
- ¼ cup all-purpose flour
- 1¼ cups beef broth
- ½ cup red wine
- ¾ teaspoon dried thyme
- 12 oz. portobello mushrooms, cut into ¾-inch cubes
- 1½ cups pearl onions, peeled, or frozen whole small onions, thawed
- ¾ cup diced carrots
- ¾ cup peas

CRUST
- 1½ pounds russet potatoes, peeled, cut into chunks
- 1½ teaspoons salt
- ¼ cup sour cream
- ¼ cup chopped fresh chives or green onion tops
- ⅛ teaspoon freshly ground pepper

1. Heat oil in nonreactive Dutch oven or large pot over medium-high heat. Add beef in batches; cook until brown. Sprinkle with flour, stir to coat. Add broth, wine and thyme; stir, scraping bottom to remove any brown bits. Add mushrooms and onions. Bring to a boil; reduce heat to low and maintain a gentle boil. Cook 1½ hours. (Mixture should be thick and reduced to about one-third of original volume.) Add carrots during last 30 minutes of cooking; add peas during last 10 minutes of cooking.

2. Meanwhile, place potatoes in large saucepan; add enough water to cover. Add 1 teaspoon of the salt. Bring to a boil over medium heat; cook 20 to 25 minutes or until potatoes are tender. Drain, reserving cooking water. Put potatoes in large bowl; mash. Stir in sour cream and enough cooking water to make potatoes fluffy and smooth. Stir in chives, remaining ½ teaspoon salt and pepper.

3. Heat broiler. When beef mixture is tender, transfer to deep 9-inch pie plate. Top with potatoes; broil 5 minutes or until browned.

6 servings.
Preparation time: 50 minutes. Ready to serve: 2 hours, 25 minutes.
Per serving: 365 calories, 15.5 g total fat (5 g saturated fat), 55 mg cholesterol, 675 mg sodium, 4.5 g fiber.

CAULIFLOWER AND GARBANZO BEAN TAGINE

Tagine is Morocco's version of stew. Serve this dish with Spicy Pea Pod and Orange Salad *(page 55).*

1	tablespoon vegetable oil
1	large onion, chopped
2	teaspoons paprika
1	teaspoon ground cumin
1/2	teaspoon ground ginger
1/4	teaspoon salt
1/8	teaspoon cayenne
2	cups *Light Vegetable Stock* (page 60) or water
2	tablespoons lemon juice
1	(2- to 2 1/2-lb.) cauliflower, florets only
1	stick cinnamon
1	(15-oz.) can garbanzo beans, rinsed, drained
1	red bell pepper, seeded, cut into 1/2-inch pieces
2	tablespoons chopped fresh cilantro

❶ Heat oil in nonreactive Dutch oven or large pot over medium-high heat until hot. Add onion; sauté 5 to 7 minutes or until lightly browned. Stir in paprika, cumin, ginger, salt and cayenne; cook 30 to 60 minutes or until fragrant. Stir in stock and lemon juice; add cauliflower and cinnamon stick. Bring to boil; reduce heat to medium-low. Cook, covered, 10 minutes.

❷ Add beans and bell pepper; reduce heat to low. Cook, covered, an additional 10 minutes. Remove cinnamon stick; sprinkle with cilantro. Serve over cooked couscous, if desired.

6 servings.
Preparation time: 15 minutes.
Ready to serve: 50 minutes.

Per serving: 140 calories, 4 g total fat (.5 g saturated fat), 0 mg cholesterol, 240 mg sodium, 5.5 g fiber.

CHICKEN, VEGETABLE AND CORNBREAD COBBLER

The Cajun seasoning adds a spicy kick to this savory cobbler. To make this dish vegetarian, substitute one (15-oz.) can red or kidney beans, rinsed and drained, for the chicken.

3	tablespoons vegetable oil
1	lb. boneless skinless chicken thighs, cubed
1	large onion, chopped
1/3	cup all-purpose flour
2 to 3	teaspoons Cajun seasoning
1 3/4	cups water or *Light Vegetable Stock* (page 60)
1 1/2	cups corn
1 1/2	cups lima beans
2	medium carrots, peeled, sliced
1	(8.5-oz.) box cornbread mix
1/3	cup milk
1	egg

❶ Heat oven to 400°F. Heat oil in large skillet over medium-high heat until hot. Add chicken and onion; sauté 3 to 4 minutes or until tender. Sprinkle with flour and Cajun seasoning; stir to combine. Whisk in water. Bring to a boil; add corn, beans and carrots. Bring to a simmer; reduce heat to low. Cook, covered, 15 minutes, stirring occasionally. Pour into 8 x 12-inch (2-quart) baking dish.

❷ In medium bowl, combine cornbread mix, milk and egg; mix well. Drop by spoonfuls over surface of chicken mixture; spread gently to cover, leaving 1/2-inch border around edge. Bake 20 minutes or until cornbread is golden and filling is bubbly.

6 servings.
Preparation time: 16 minutes. Ready to serve: 55 minutes.

Per serving: 480 calories, 21 g total fat (6 g saturated fat), 90 mg cholesterol, 595 mg sodium, 7 g fiber.

CHORIZO CHILI

Chorizo is a type of sausage found in Mexican and southwestern cooking. Feel free to substitute a spicy Italian sausage if unavailable. Use canned tomatoes for convenience or when fresh ones are out of season. To make this dish vegetarian, substitute one (15-oz.) can of pinto or garbanzo beans for the chorizo, and add a chopped chipotle chile or jalepeño pepper to liven up the seasoning.

1 tablespoon vegetable oil

1/2 lb. chorizo or other spicy sausage, sliced

1 large onion, chopped (1 cup)

1 green pepper, chopped

1 tablespoon minced garlic

1 (28-oz.) can diced tomatoes, undrained, or 2 pounds chopped fresh tomatoes

1 (15-oz.) can kidney beans, rinsed, drained

1 (14.5-oz) can beef broth

2 tablespoons chili powder

1 teaspoon ground cumin

1/2 teaspoon dried oregano

1/8 teaspoon cayenne

1 cup corn

❶ Heat nonreactive Dutch oven or large pot over medium-high heat. Add oil; heat until hot. Add chorizo; sauté 2 to 3 minutes or until chorizo begins to brown. Add onion, green pepper and garlic; sauté 3 to 4 minutes or until vegetables begin to soften. Add tomatoes, beans, broth, chili powder, cumin and oregano; mix well. Bring to a boil; reduce heat to low. Simmer, partially covered, 20 minutes. Add corn; cook an additional 10 minutes.

4 to 6 servings.
Preparation time: 15 minutes.
Ready to serve: 40 minutes.

Per serving: 475 calories, 27 g total fat (9 g saturated fat), 50 mg cholesterol, 1755 mg sodium, 9 g fiber.

INDIAN ROOT VEGETABLE CURRY

Curries are synonymous with India and the word originates from the Indian word "karhi," meaning sauce. In other parts of the world, curries are often erroneously considered a spice or a blend of spices, a concept that is non-existent in India. Versions of this root vegetable stew are found all over southern India, and this curry derives its flavors from chiles, coconut and cilantro. If you can't find unsweetened coconut, substitute the sweetened kind but rinse it thoroughly under cold water first, then pat it dry.

1½	cups water
1	medium white or red potato, peeled, cut into ½-inch cubes
1	medium sweet potato, peeled, cut into ½-inch cubes
1	medium carrot, peeled, cut into ½-inch cubes
½	cup chopped red onion
1	cup freshly grated coconut (or ½ cup dried unsweetened coconut, shredded)
3 to 4	fresh serrano chilies
½	cup fresh cilantro
1	medium tomato, cut into ½-inch cubes
1	cup peas
1	teaspoon vegetable oil
1	teaspoon ground cumin
1	teaspoon salt

❶ In medium saucepan, bring water, white potato, sweet potato, carrot and onion to a boil over medium-high heat. Reduce heat to low; simmer, covered, 6 to 8 minutes or until vegetables are al dente.

❷ Meanwhile, place coconut, chiles, and cilantro in food processor; process until chiles and cilantro are finely minced. Add coconut mixture, tomato and peas to potato mixture; mix well. Simmer, uncovered, 4 to 6 minutes or until peas are cooked through.

❸ Heat oil in small skillet over medium-high heat until hot; add cumin seed. Cook 15 to 20 seconds. Add oil mixture to vegetable mixture; season with salt. Mix well. Serve with cooked rice, if desired.

6 servings.
Preparation time: 18 minutes. Ready to serve: 40 minutes.

Per serving: 135 calories, 5.5 g total fat (4 g saturated fat), 0 mg cholesterol, 425 mg sodium, 4.5 g fiber.

FOUR SEASONS PIZZA

This is a classic Italian pizza with the four sections representing the four seasons. Use this recipe as a base for any vegetable topping you choose.

CRUST
- 1 cup lukewarm water (105°F to 115°F)
- 1 (1/4-oz.) pkg. active dry yeast
- 3 cups all-purpose flour
- 2 teaspoons sugar
- 1/2 teaspoon salt
- 1 tablespoon olive oil

TOPPING
- 1 (8-oz.) can tomato sauce
- 4 oz. white mushrooms, thinly sliced
- 1 tablespoon olive oil
- 1/2 green bell pepper, thinly sliced
- 1 (6.5-oz.) jar marinated artichoke hearts, drained, coarsely chopped
- 2 to 3 plum tomatoes, thinly sliced
- 2 cups (8 oz.) shredded mozzarella cheese

❶ Heat oven to 450°F. Lightly spray 2 baking sheets or 2 (14-inch) pizza pans with nonstick cooking spray. Combine water and yeast in small bowl; let sit 5 minutes. In large bowl, combine 2 1/2 cups of the flour, sugar and salt; mix well. Add yeast mixture and oil to flour mixture; stir to make a soft dough. Dust work surface with remaining 1/2 cup flour. Turn dough out onto floured surface, knead until smooth dough forms, adding additional flour if needed to prevent sticking.

❷ Divide dough in half; shape each half into disk. Roll each disk into a 14-inch round. Place on baking sheets; spread each with half of tomato sauce. In medium bowl, toss mushrooms with 1 tablespoon oil. Cover 1/4 of each pizza with mushrooms, 1/4 with bell pepper, 1/4 with artichoke hearts and 1/4 with tomatoes. Sprinkle each pizza with 1 cup of the cheese. Bake 10 to 12 minutes or until browned and crisp.

2 (14-inch) pizzas, 8 slices each.
Preparation time: 25 minutes. Ready to serve: 43 minutes.

Per slice: 420 calories, 12.5 g total fat (5 g saturated fat), 20 mg cholesterol, 705 mg sodium, 4 g fiber.

SQUASH RAVIOLI WITH RED PEPPER SAUCE

Cooked squash often has excess moisture. Place the squash in a fine strainer for 15 minutes before use, gently turning from time to time, to allow it to drain.

SAUCE

2	red bell peppers, halved
1/2	cup reduced-sodium chicken broth or 1/3 cup *Light Vegetable Stock* (page 60)
2	tablespoons sour cream
1/4	teaspoon salt

FILLING

1	cup drained cooked squash (such as butternut)*
3/4	cup (3 oz.) freshly grated Parmesan cheese
1/4	cup dry bread crumbs
1	egg
3/4	teaspoon dried sage
1/8	teaspoon freshly ground pepper

PASTA**

1 1/3 to 1 1/2	cups all-purpose flour
2	teaspoons salt
2	eggs

❶ Heat broiler. Line shallow baking pan with foil. Place bell peppers on pan skin side up; broil 4 to 6 inches from heat 7 to 10 minutes or until blackened. Remove. Place in bowl; cover. Let sit 5 minutes. Remove charred skin and seeds. Place bell peppers and broth in food processor or blender; puree. Set aside.

❷ In medium bowl, combine squash, cheese, breadcrumbs, egg, sage and pepper. Set aside.

❸ In food processor, combine 1/3 cup of the flour and 2 teaspoons of the salt. With motor running, add eggs one at a time; process until mixture forms small grains of pasta. (Dough should not be sticky. Add additional flour if necessary.) Pat dough into ball; divide into 4 pieces.

❹ Work with one piece of dough at a time, keeping remaining dough covered with towel. Roll dough into cylinder; flatten to about 1/2-inch thickness. Using hand-cranked pasta machine, feed dough through using widest setting. Feed dough through again using next to the lowest setting, dusting as necessary with small amount of flour to prevent dough from sticking. On very lightly floured surface, trim dough to 4-inch-wide strip. Place ¹/₂ tablespoon squash filling every 2 inches along right side of strip until there are 12 circles of filling. Using finger dipped in water, dampen dough around filling. Fold dough in half lengthwise; press around filling to seal. Cut into 12 squares trimming away excess dough. Set aside on very lightly floured surface. Repeat with remaining dough.

⑤ Bring large pot of water to a boil. Add remaining 2 teaspoons salt. Add ravioli; cook 3 to 4 minutes. Drain.

⑥ While ravioli are cooking, place bell pepper mixture in medium saucepan. Bring to a boil over medium-low heat. Remove from heat; stir in sour cream and 2 teaspoons salt. Reserve ¹/₄ cup sauce. Divide remaining sauce among 4 plates, creating ring of sauce on each plate. Place drained ravioli in center of rings. Garnish center of each with 1 tablespoon of sauce.

TIP *To cook squash, heat oven to 375°F. Line baking sheet with foil; lightly grease. Cut squash in half lengthwise; place on baking sheet. Bake 1 hour or until tender. Scoop flesh from shell; freeze excess squash in plastic freezer bag for another use.

TIP **Gyoza or wonton skins can be substituted for freshly made pasta. Use 48 skins. Place 1 tablespoon of filling in center of each of 24 skins. Dampen edge of each with water; top with remaining skins. Press to seal. Cook in boiling salted water 2 to 3 minutes.

4 servings.
Preparation time: 42 minutes. Ready to serve: 2 hours.
Per serving: 385 calories, 12.5 g total fat (6.5 g saturated fat), 180 mg cholesterol, 1875 mg sodium, 3 g fiber.

PEAS, PEARL ONIONS, SMOKED TURKEY AND PARMESAN PASTA

Frozen vegetables are the first choice to make this dish quickly. To make a vegetarian version, substitute another vegetable for the turkey (perhaps asparagus or carrots) and grate a smoked cheese (such as provolone) over the finished dish.

16 to 20 frozen small whole onions (or skinned fresh pearl onions)
1 cup reduced-sodium chicken broth
1 cup frozen or fresh shelled peas
1/2 lb. smoked turkey, cut into 1/2-inch pieces
1/2 cup whipping cream
1/8 teaspoon freshly ground pepper
1 (9-oz.) pkg. fresh or dried fettuccini
1/4 cup (1 oz.) freshly grated Parmesan cheese

❶ In large skillet over medium-low heat, cook onions and broth, covered, 10 minutes or until onions are tender. Uncover; add peas, turkey, cream and pepper. Increase heat to medium-high; bring to boil. Cook 5 to 8 minutes or until peas are tender and sauce has reduced slightly.

❷ Meanwhile, cook fettuccine according to package directions. Drain. Place sauce in large shallow bowl. Stir in 2 tablespoons of the cheese. Add fettuccine; toss to coat. Sprinkle with remaining 2 tablespoons cheese; toss. Serve with additional cheese if desired.

4 servings.
Preparation time: 5 minutes. Ready to serve: 20 minutes.

Per serving: 460 calories, 17 g total fat (8.5 g saturated fat), 12.5 mg cholesterol, 1135 mg sodium, 4.5 g fiber.

TABBOULEH FETA POCKETS

Add bits of cooked lamb or chicken to this sandwich, if desired, or serve the filling as a salad accompaniment.

- 1   cup water
- 1/2   cup bulgur
- 1   medium tomato, chopped
- 1/2   medium cucumber, peeled, chopped (about 1/2 cup)
- 2   oz. feta cheese, crumbled (about 1/2 cup)
- 1/4   cup chopped green onions
- 1/4   cup chopped fresh mint
- 1/4   cup chopped fresh parsley
- 2   tablespoons sliced ripe olives
- 2   tablespoons lemon juice
- 2   tablespoons extra-virgin olive oil
- 1/4   teaspoon salt
- 1/8   teaspoon freshly ground pepper
- 3   pitas

❶ In small saucepan over medium heat, bring water and bulgur to a boil. Reduce heat to low; simmer 5 minutes. Remove from heat; cover. Let sit 5 minutes; cool.

❷ In medium bowl, combine bulgur, tomato, cucumber, cheese, onions, mint, parsley and olives. In small bowl, combine lemon juice, oil, salt and pepper. Toss with bulgur mixture. Refrigerate, covered, until ready to serve.

❸ Cut pitas in half; fill pockets evenly with mixture.

6 servings.
Preparation time: 15 minutes.
Ready to serve: 30 minutes.

Per serving: 180 calories, 7.5 g total fat (2 g saturated fat), 10 mg cholesterol, 355 mg sodium, 3.5 g fiber.

VEGETARIAN GUMBO

Making a roux involves cooking butter or oil and flour together and is a common technique in recipes from France and Louisiana. What sets the Louisiana technique apart is the custom of browning the roux. This adds a rich and nutty flavor to the finished dish.

1/4 cup vegetable oil
1/4 cup all-purpose flour
1 large onion, chopped
1 large green bell pepper, chopped
1 1/2 teaspoons minced garlic
1 lb. tomatoes, coarsely chopped
2 cups water
2 cups sliced okra
1 (15-oz.) can kidney beans, rinsed, drained
2 teaspoons Cajun seasoning
1/2 teaspoon salt
1/8 teaspoon freshly ground black pepper
1 bunch collard greens (about 1/2-lb.), stemmed, coarsely chopped

❶ Heat oil in nonreactive Dutch oven or large pot over medium-high heat until hot. Stir in flour; cook about 5 minutes or until flour turns to a medium brown, stirring constantly. Stir in onion, bell pepper and garlic; cook 3 to 4 minutes or until vegetables begin to soften, stirring constantly.

❷ Add tomatoes, water, okra, beans, Cajun seasoning, salt and pepper; stir to combine. Reduce heat to low; cook, partially covered, 30 minutes. Add collard greens; cook an additional 10 minutes. Serve over cooked rice, if desired.

6 (1-cup) servings.
Preparation time: 25 minutes. Ready to serve: 1 hour, 5 minutes.
Per serving: 200 calories, 10 g total fat (1.5 g saturated fat), 0 mg cholesterol, 425 mg sodium, 5.5 g fiber.

TOMATO-OLIVE RAGOUT WITH POLENTA

To peel tomatoes, bring a large pot of water to a boil. Drop tomatoes in water for approximately one minute. Plunge into cold water. Skins should come off easily with a sharp knife. Kalamata olives are dark, Greek olives packed in brine. If possible, buy them already pitted. Otherwise, press down on the olive with the flat side of a large knife blade; this crushes the olive and loosens the pit.

RAGOUT
 2 tablespoons olive oil
 1 large onion, sliced
 1 medium bulb fennel, fronds removed, sliced
 1 tablespoon minced garlic
 8 oz. crimini mushrooms, sliced
 2 lb. tomatoes, peeled, cut into 1-inch pieces
 1/2 cup pitted Kalamata olives
 1/4 teaspoon salt

POLENTA
 3 cups water
 1/2 teaspoon salt
 1/2 teaspoon dried thyme
 3/4 cup polenta style cornmeal

1 Heat oil in nonreactive Dutch oven or large pot over medium heat until hot. Add onion and fennel; sauté 4 to 5 minutes or until onion and fennel begin to soften. Add garlic; cook 1 minute. Add mushrooms; sauté an additional 4 to 5 minutes. Add tomatoes, olives and 1/4 teaspoon salt; cook 20 to 25 minutes or until tomatoes have reduced and ragout has thickened, stirring occasionally.

2 Lightly grease 8-inch square pan. In medium saucepan, bring water, 1/2 teaspoon salt and thyme to a boil over medium heat. Slowly whisk in cornmeal. Reduce heat to low; cook 5 to 10 minutes or until mixture thickens and polenta begins to pull away from sides of pan, stirring constantly. Pour into pan; let sit until firm.

3 Cut into fourths; cut each fourth into triangles. Place two triangles on each plate. Top with 1/4 of ragout.

4 servings.
Preparation time: 35 minutes. Ready to serve: 45 minutes.

Per serving: 270 calories, 10.5 g total fat (1.5 g saturated fat), 0 mg cholesterol, 650 mg sodium, 7.5 g fiber.

WILD MUSHROOM LASAGNA

Cooking the mushrooms with the soaking liquid from the dried mushrooms intensifies the porcini flavor.

- 1 (1-oz.) pkg. dried porcini mushrooms
- 1 cup very hot water
- 1 tablespoon vegetable oil
- 1 small onion, chopped
- 1 tablespoon minced garlic
- 1 lb. assorted fresh mushrooms (such as white, crimini and chanterelle), chopped
- 3/4 cup dry red wine
- 1/4 teaspoon dried thyme
- 1/2 teaspoon salt
- 1/4 teaspoon freshly ground pepper
- 3 tablespoons water
- 5 teaspoons all-purpose flour
- 1 (15-oz.) container ricotta cheese or dry curd cottage cheese
- 1/4 cup (1-oz.) freshly grated Parmesan cheese
- 1/4 cup chopped chives or green onion tops
- 1 egg
- 6 cooked lasagna noodles
- 4 oz. grated mozzarella cheese (about 1 cup)

❶ Soak dried mushrooms in hot water 30 minutes; remove mushrooms. Strain soaking liquid through coffee filter; reserve liquid. Chop mushrooms; set aside.

❷ Heat oven to 350°F. Heat oil in large skillet over medium-high heat until hot. Add onion; sauté 3 to 4 minutes or until softened. Add garlic; sauté 1 minute or until fragrant. Add 1 lb. mushrooms; sauté 5 to 8 minutes or until tender. Add wine, porcini mushrooms, reserved soaking liquid, thyme, 1/4 teaspoon of the salt and 1/8 teaspoon of the pepper. Reduce heat to medium-low; simmer 10 minutes.

❸ In small bowl, whisk together water and flour. Whisk flour mixture into mushroom mixture; simmer 2 to 3 minutes or until slightly thickened. Meanwhile, in medium bowl, combine ricotta cheese, Parmesan cheese, chives, egg and remaining 1/4 teaspoon salt and 1/8 teaspoon pepper.

④ To assemble, spread half of mushroom mixture on bottom of 8 x 12-inch (or 9 x 13-inch) baking dish. Arrange 3 of the cooked lasagna noodles on top of mushroom mixture; spoon and spread cheese mixture over noodles. Top with 3 remaining noodles; finish topping with remaining mushroom mixture. Sprinkle top with mozzarella cheese.

⑤ Bake, covered, 30 to 35 minutes or until heated through and bubbly. Uncover; let sit 10 minutes before serving.

6 servings.
Preparation time: 30 minutes. Ready to serve: 1 hour, 40 minutes.

Per serving: 325 calories, 14 g total fat (7 g saturated fat), 70 mg cholesterol, 565 mg sodium, 2 g fiber.

ZUCCHINI AND TOMATO FRITTATA

Serve this dish for brunch along with Frosty Marys *(page 24). Add* Corn and Barley Salad *(page 43) plus your favorite muffin to round out the menu.*

3 tablespoons olive oil
1 large onion, chopped
1 small zucchini, halved, sliced
1 small summer squash, halved, sliced
2 teaspoons minced garlic
8 eggs
3/4 teaspoon dried oregano
1/2 teaspoon dried dill weed
1/2 teaspoon salt
1/4 teaspoon freshly ground pepper
2 oz. crumbled feta cheese (about 1/2 cup)
1 medium tomato, sliced

❶ Heat oil in large nonstick skillet over medium-high heat until hot. Add onion; sauté 4 to 5 minutes or until softened. Add zucchini, squash and garlic; sauté 5 minutes or until zucchini and squash have softened.

❷ In medium bowl, combine eggs, oregano, dill weed, salt and pepper; beat well. Reduce heat to low; add egg mixture to squash mixture. Sprinkle with cheese. Cover and cook 5 minutes, pushing egg back from sides of pan. Occasionally tip pan and cut through egg mixture with spatula to allow uncooked egg to run to bottom of pan. Top with sliced tomato; continue to cook, covered, 5 to 7 minutes, occasionally pushing and tipping eggs.

❸ When egg mixture has set, slide onto serving platter.

4 servings.
Preparation time: 30 minutes. Ready to serve: 30 minutes.
Per serving: 310 calories, 23.5 g total fat (6.5 g saturated fat), 440 mg cholesterol, 580 mg sodium, 2 g fiber.

DESSERTS

In many people's estimation, "Life is short; eat dessert first" might be a better thought than "Eat your vegetables." This chapter proves you can do both. Enjoy!

Maple-Pumpkin Cheesecake, page 126

MAPLE-PUMPKIN CHEESECAKE

To save time, serve this cheesecake with purchased caramel topping or simply top with a spoonful of lightly sweetened whipped cream.

CRUST
3/4   cup chopped walnuts
3/4   cup graham cracker crumbs
1/4   cup sugar
1/4   cup butter, melted, cooled

FILLING
3   (8-oz.) pkg. cream cheese, softened
1   cup packed light brown sugar
4   eggs, room temperature
1/4   cup sugar
3   tablespoons all-purpose flour
1 1/2   teaspoons ground cinnamon
1/2   teaspoon ground ginger
1/4   teaspoon ground nutmeg
1   (8-oz.) container sour cream
3/4   teaspoon maple extract
2   cups cooked pumpkin* (or 1 (15-oz.) can)

TOPPING
3/4   cup maple syrup
1/2   cup packed light brown sugar
1/2   cup apple cider or water

❶ Heat oven to 350°F. In food processor, pulse together walnuts and graham cracker crumbs until finely ground. Add 1/4 cup sugar; pulse to combine. Add butter; pulse to combine. Pat mixture over bottom and 1 inch up sides of 10-inch springform pan. Bake 10 minutes. Remove from oven; let cool.

❷ In large bowl, beat cream cheese at medium speed until soft. Add 1 cup brown sugar; beat until very soft. Add eggs one at a time, beating only until combined after each addition. In medium bowl, whisk together 1/4 cup sugar, flour, cinnamon, ginger and nutmeg. Whisk in sour cream and maple extract. Beat sour cream mixture into cream cheese mixture at low speed just until combined. Stir in pumpkin. Pour into springform pan. Place springform pan on baking sheet; bake 55 to 65 minutes or until center is just set. (Center should be less set than edges and will move when pan is tapped.) Cool on wire rack 1 hour. Cover; refrigerate 3 to 4 hours or overnight.

③ To make topping, place maple syrup, brown sugar and apple cider in medium saucepan. Cook over medium heat until mixture comes to a boil, stirring occasionally. Continue to boil without stirring 10 minutes or until mixture has reduced and slightly thickened. To serve, spoon sauce over cheesecake.

TIP *To cook pumpkin, halve 2½- to 3-lb. pumpkin lengthwise. Place on foil-lined shallow pan; bake at 375°F for 1 hour or until very soft. Cool. Remove seeds; scrape out flesh. Place flesh in fine strainer over small bowl 15 minutes, to allow to drain, turning occasionally.

12 servings.
Preparation time: 25 minutes. Ready to serve: 6 hours, 40 minutes.
Per serving: 580 calories, 34.5 g total fat (18.5 g saturated fat), 155 mg cholesterol, 265 mg sodium, 2 g fiber.

TRIPLE CHOCOLATE ZUCCHINI CAKE

Zucchini is the magic ingredient in this yummy cake. Hidden in all the chocolate, it adds moistness and body.

CAKE
- 1/4 cup milk
- 1/4 cup orange juice
- 1 tablespoon grated orange peel
- 3/4 cup butter, softened
- 2 cups sugar
- 3 eggs
- 2 1/4 cups all-purpose flour
- 1/2 cup unsweetened cocoa
- 2 teaspoons baking powder
- 1 teaspoon ground cinnamon
- 3/4 teaspoon baking soda
- 1/2 teaspoon salt
- 2 cups shredded unpeeled zucchini
- 1 cup (6 oz.) semisweet chocolate chips

GLAZE
- 3 oz. milk chocolate, chopped
- 5 teaspoons orange juice

❶ Heat oven to 350°F. Spray 10-inch Bundt pan with nonstick cooking spray; dust with flour. In small bowl, combine milk, orange juice and orange peel. Set aside.

❷ Beat butter in large bowl at medium speed until creamy. Add sugar; beat until fluffy. Add eggs one at a time, beating well after each addition.

❸ In another large bowl, sift together flour, cocoa, baking powder, cinnamon, baking soda and salt. Beat half of flour mixture into butter mixture at low speed just until combined. Add milk mixture; mix just until combined. Add remaining flour mixture; mix until combined. Stir in zucchini and chocolate chips.

④ Spoon batter into pan. Bake 55 to 60 minutes or until top feels firm to touch and toothpick inserted in center comes out clean. Cool in pan on wire rack 15 minutes. Invert onto rack; cool completely.

⑤ In double broiler over barely simmering water, melt chocolate and orange juice. Stir until smooth. Drizzle over top and sides of cake.

12 servings.
Preparation time: 30 minutes. Ready to serve: 3 hours, 40 minutes.

Per serving: 460 calories, 20 g total fat (12 g saturated fat), 85 mg cholesterol, 360 mg sodium, 3.5 g fiber.

GREEN TOMATO PIE

This is an old-fashioned dessert designed to use up green tomatoes at season's end. Its resemblance to classic apple pie is uncanny.

CRUST

2¼	cups all-purpose flour
½	teaspoon salt
¾	cup unsalted butter, cut into ½-inch cubes
2	tablespoons shortening or unsalted butter
5 to 6	tablespoons ice water

FILLING

4	cups green tomatoes, sliced ¼- to ½-inch thick
2	cups peeled apples, sliced ¼- to ½-inch thick
1	teaspoon grated lime peel
1	cup sugar
¼	cup all-purpose flour
1	teaspoon ground cinnamon

❶ Combine 2¼ cups flour and ½ teaspoon salt in medium mixing bowl. Add butter and shortening; toss to coat. Work with pastry blender or 2 knives, work butter and shortening into flour until mixture resembles coarse meal with some larger pieces of butter remaining. Toss with just enough water to form a ball. Divide dough into 2 pieces; roll each into a ball, one slightly larger than the other. Shape dough into flat disk; wrap in plastic wrap. Refrigerate 1 hour.

❷ Heat oven to 425°F. Combine tomatoes, apples and lime peel in large mixing bowl. In small bowl, stir together sugar, ¼ cup flour and cinnamon. Toss with apple mixture.

❸ Roll out larger disk of dough to ⅛-inch thickness. Line 9-inch pie pan with dough. Fill with apple mixture. Roll out small disk of dough to ⅛-inch thickness; place over apple mixture. Pinch edges of crust together to seal; trim overhang. Cut slits in top to allow steam to escape.

❹ Bake at 425°F for 15 minutes. Reduce oven temperature to 375°F; continue baking an additional 40 to 50 minutes or until juices are bubbly. If pie crust appears to be browning too quickly, cover edges with foil to protect crust.

8 servings.
Preparation time: 30 minutes. Ready to serve: 4 hours.

Per serving: 455 calories, 21 g total fat (11.5 g saturated fat), 45 mg cholesterol, 155 mg sodium, 2.5 g fiber.

$\mathcal{A}$PPLE AND WALNUT CAKE WITH CARAMEL SAUCE

Beets add sweetness and color to this moist fall cake.

CAKE
1/2	cup unsalted butter, softened
13/4	cups plus 1/3 cup sugar
3	eggs
11/2	cups unsweetened applesauce
3	cups all-purpose flour
11/2	teaspoons baking soda
21/2	teaspoons ground cinnamon
1	teaspoon salt
1/2	teaspoon ground nutmeg
1/2	teaspoon ground allspice
1	medium Granny Smith apple, peeled, chopped (about 1 cup)
1	beet, cooked, peeled, cut into 1/4-inch pieces (about 1 cup)
1/2	cup chopped walnuts

SAUCE
1/2	cup unsalted butter
11/2	cups packed light brown sugar
1	cup heavy cream

❶ Heat oven to 350°F. Grease and flour a 13 x 9-inch pan. Beat 1/2 cup butter in large mixer bowl at medium speed until creamy. Add 13/4 cups sugar and beat until fluffy. Add eggs one at a time, beating well after each addition. Mixture will look curdled. Stir in applesauce.

❷ In large bowl, sift together flour, baking soda, 11/2 teaspoons of the cinnamon, salt, nutmeg and allspice. Add to applesauce mixture; beat at low speed until combined. Increase speed to medium; beat 30 seconds. Stir in apples, beets and walnuts. Spread into pan.

❸ In small bowl, combine remaining 1/3 cup sugar and 1 teaspoon cinnamon; sprinkle over surface of cake. Bake 60 to 65 minutes or until toothpick inserted in center comes out clean. Cool on wire rack.

❹ In medium saucepan, melt 1/2 cup butter over medium heat until medium brown in color. Add brown sugar and cream; bring to a boil, stirring constantly. Boil 1 minute. Remove from heat; cool slightly.

❺ Place pool of caramel sauce on each plate; top with piece of cake.

15 servings.
Preparation time: 30 minutes. Ready to serve: 4 hours, 30 minutes.

Per serving: 495 calories, 21 g total fat (11.5 g saturated fat), 95 mg cholesterol, 315 mg sodium, 1.5 g fiber.

CARROT AND CARDAMOM COOKIES

Cardamom and almond are traditional Scandinavian flavorings. Here they team up with orange flecks of carrot and green pistachios for great taste and visual appeal.

1/2 cup butter
1 cup sugar
1 cup packed brown sugar
2 eggs
1/2 teaspoon almond extract
31/4 cups all-purpose flour
2 teaspoons ground cardamom
1 teaspoon baking soda
1/4 teaspoon salt
1 cup shredded carrots
1/2 cup chopped pistachios

❶ Heat oven to 375°F. Line baking sheet with parchment paper. In large bowl, beat butter, sugar and brown sugar at medium speed until well combined. Add eggs 1 at a time, beating well after each addition. Add almond extract; mix well. In another large bowl, sift together flour, cardamom, baking soda and salt. Add to butter mixture; beat at low speed just until combined. Stir in carrots and pistachios.

❷ Form dough into 1-inch balls. Place on baking sheet. Flatten with tines of fork dipped in sugar. Bake 9 to 11 minutes or until lightly browned. Cool on wire racks. Store in tightly covered containers.

5 dozen cookies.
Preparation time: 45 minutes. Ready to serve: 1 hour, 30 minutes.
Per cookie: 75 calories, 2.5 g total fat (1 g saturated fat), 10 mg cholesterol, 45 mg sodium, .5 g fiber.

PUMPKIN-PECAN BARS

A cross between pumpkin and pecan pie, these bars are great to bake-and-take.

1³/4   cups all-purpose flour
3/4   cup butter
1/3   cup powdered sugar
2   cups cooked pumpkin* (or 1 (15-oz.) can)
1   cup sugar
1   cup dark corn syrup
3   eggs
2   tablespoons butter, melted, cooled
1   teaspoon vanilla
1/2   teaspoon ground cinnamon
1/4   teaspoon salt
1¹/2   cups chopped pecans

❶ Heat oven to 350°F. In food processor, pulse together 1¹/2 cups of the flour, 3/4 cup butter and powdered sugar. (Mixture will be dry.) Place mixture in 13 x 9-inch pan; press into bottom of pan. Bake 15 minutes or until lightly browned.

❷ Place pumpkin, sugar, corn syrup, eggs, melted butter and vanilla in food processor; pulse to combine. In small bowl, stir together remaining 1/4 cub flour, cinnamon and salt; add to pumpkin mixture. Pulse just until combined. Stir in pecans. Pour into crust. Bake 55 to 60 minutes or until top is no longer sticky to the touch. Cool on wire rack.

TIP *See *Maple-Pumpkin Cheesecake* (page 126) for directions on cooking pumpkin.

48 bars.
Preparation time: 10 minutes. Ready to serve: 4 hours.
Per bar: 120 calories, 6.5 g total fat (2.5 g saturated fat), 20 mg cholesterol, 45 mg sodium, 1 g fiber.

INEAPPLE UPSIDE-DOWN CARROT CAKE

This recipe combines two traditional American favorites — pineapple upside-down cake and carrot cake — into one fabulous dessert.

6	tablespoons butter, melted
1¹⁄₂	cups packed brown sugar
3	(8-oz.) cans pineapple slices, drained
12	maraschino cherries
1³⁄₄	cups sugar
1	cup vegetable oil
2	teaspoons vanilla
3	eggs
2¹⁄₂	cups all-purpose flour
2	teaspoons baking soda
1	teaspoon ground cinnamon
³⁄₄	teaspoon salt
¹⁄₂	teaspoon ground ginger
2¹⁄₂	cups shredded carrots

❶ Heat oven to 350°F. Pour butter into 13 x 9-inch pan, brushing bottom and sides with butter. Sprinkle brown sugar evenly over bottom of pan; top with pineapple slices. Place maraschino cherry in center of each pineapple slice.

❷ In large bowl, combine sugar, oil, vanilla and eggs; beat well. In another large bowl, sift together flour, baking soda, cinnamon, salt and ginger. Add flour mixture to sugar mixture; mix well. Stir in carrots.

❸ Pour batter into pan. Bake 55 to 60 minutes or until cake springs back when lightly touched in center. Cool on wire rack 5 minutes. Invert onto serving platter; cool completely.

12 servings.
Preparation time: 20 minutes. Ready to serve: 3 hours, 20 minutes.

Per serving: 580 calories, 25.5 g total fat (6.5 g saturated fat), 70 mg cholesterol, 430 mg sodium, 2 g fiber.

SQUASH GINGERBREAD

The squash adds moistness and flavor to this cold-weather favorite. Serve it with hot caramel sauce or with a scoop of vanilla ice cream.

1/2	cup pureed cooked squash*
1/2	cup packed light brown sugar
1/3	cup vegetable oil
1	egg
1/2	cup light molasses
1/2	cup water
1 1/2	cups all-purpose flour
1 1/4	teaspoons ground ginger
1	teaspoon baking powder
1/2	teaspoon baking soda
1/2	teaspoon ground cinnamon
1/4	teaspoon salt
1/4	teaspoon ground cloves

1 Heat oven to 350°F. Grease bottom of 8-inch square pan. In medium bowl, beat together squash, brown sugar and oil. Beat in egg, molasses and water. In another medium bowl, sift together flour, ginger, baking powder, baking soda, cinnamon, salt and cloves. Add flour mixture to squash mixture; mix.

2 Pour into pan. Bake 40 to 45 minutes or until top is firm and toothpick inserted in center comes out clean.

TIP *See Squash Ravioli with Red Pepper Sauce (page 112) for instructions on cooking squash.

9 servings.
Preparation time: 10 minutes. Ready to serve: 3 hours.
Per serving: 255 calories, 9 g total fat (1.5 g saturated fat), 25 mg cholesterol, 210 mg sodium, 1 g fiber.

SWEET POTATO CREME BRULEE

Brown sugar is the best sugar choice for making crème brûlée under the broiler. If you own a small torch, sold in specialty cookware stores, substitute granulated sugar instead and follow manufacturer's directions to use the torch.

1	cup cooked sweet potato*
1/2	cup sugar
2	cups half-and-half
4	egg yolks
2	eggs
2	tablespoons orange liqueur
1	tablespoon finely grated orange peel
1/4	teaspoon ground nutmeg
1/4	cup packed brown sugar

❶ Heat oven to 350°F. Place sweet potato and sugar in food processor; pulse to form a smooth puree, scraping sides as necessary. Pulse in half-and-half just until combined; pulse in egg yolks and eggs just until combined. Strain into large bowl.

❷ Stir in orange liqueur, orange peel and nutmeg. Pour into 6 (6-oz.) custard cups; place in 13 x 9-inch pan. Add enough boiling water to pan to come halfway up sides of custard cups. Bake 30 to 35 minutes or until centers are just set. Cool on wire rack 30 minutes. Refrigerate several hours or overnight.

❸ Before serving, heat broiler. Press 2 teaspoons brown sugar through strainer over surface of each custard cup. Spread to evenly cover surface. Place custard cups in shallow pan; broil approximately 2 minutes or until brown sugar has melted. (Crème brûlée can be caramelized up to 2 hours ahead; cover and refrigerate.)

TIP *To cook sweet potato, place on baking sheet; cook at 400°F for 1 hour or until flesh is soft.

6 servings.
Preparation time: 25 minutes. Ready to serve: 4 hours, 10 minutes.
Per serving: 320 calories, 14.5 g total fat (7.5 g saturated fat), 240 mg cholesterol, 65 mg sodium, .5 g fiber.

Glossary

ARTICHOKES: A member of the thistle family, artichokes are at their peak in spring. California is our biggest producer. Available in many forms, baby artichokes are eaten whole. For mature artichokes, the edible portions are its heart, bottom and the base of its leaves. Look for unblemished, heavy artichokes with tight leaves. Refrigerate, unwashed, in a plastic bag for several days. Frozen or canned artichoke hearts or bottoms make acceptable substitutions. One cooked artichoke contains 531 mg vitamin A, .33 mg vitamin B-6, 30 mg vitamin C, 153 mg folic acid, 135 mg calcium and 3.87 mg iron.

ASPARAGUS: A member of the lily family, asparagus is a spring vegetable. It is usually found as green spears or sometimes purple, although European asparagus is often white. Early asparagus is pencil-thin but appears later with thicker spears. Look for smooth, firm stalks and closed, tight tips. Store in the refrigerator upright in an inch or two of water, covered in plastic or simply wrapped airtight, for several days. Best fresh. One half-cup of cooked, fresh asparagus contains 485 mg

vitamin A, .11 mg vitamin B-6, 10 mg of vitamin C and 131 mg folic acid.

BEANS: Also called legumes, beans are grown and consumed worldwide and are a summer and fall vegetable. Consisting of a pod and inner seed, legume varieties consumed as pod and seed include

green and **yellow snap beans. Lima beans** are one of the fresh varieties consumed by eating just the seed. Dried (sometimes sold cooked and canned) varieties include **black, cannellini, chickpeas** or **garbanzo beans, Great Northern, kidney, navy, red and soy.** In fresh green and yellow beans, look for long, slender, firm, unblemished pods. Lima beans should be firm and unblemished. Store fresh beans in the refrigerator, airtight, for four to five days. Frozen green, yellow and lima beans make acceptable substitutions. One-half cup cooked, fresh green and yellow beans contains 413 mg vitamin A. One-half cup cooked lima beans contains 2.2 mg iron. Dried beans are a good source of protein.

BEETS: See root vegetables

BOK CHOY: See cabbages

BROCCOLI: A cruciferous vegetable, broccoli is related to the cabbage. Popular since Roman times, it is a cool-weather crop. Look for tight buds and firm stems. Avoid any sign of yellowing tips or woody stalks. Store in the refrigerator, airtight, for several days. Best fresh, but frozen broccoli is acceptable for cooking. One-half cup of broccoli contains 108 mg vitamin A, .11 mg vitamin B-6, 58 mg vitamin C and 36 mg calcium.

CABBAGES: Members of the *Brassica* family, the many types

of cabbages are cruciferous vegetables. They come into their own in cooler weather. The most commonly found variety in this country has tight **green** or **red**

leaves shaped in a round head. Other varieties include Asian **bok choy**, which has firm, white stalks and dark green leaves; and **Napa cabbage,** which has an oblong shape and crinkly, pale leaves with lighter centers. **Savoy cabbage** has a slightly rounded, looser head of crinkly leaves. All varieties should be crisp with no signs of wilting or blemishes and heavy for their size. Cabbages will keep in the refrigerator wrapped airtight for several days. The rounder heads will keep up to a week. Best fresh or preserved, as in sauerkraut or kimchee. One-half cup of cooked green cabbage has 99 mg vitamin A and 15 mg vitamin C; red cabbage contributes minimal amounts of vitamins. One-half cup of cooked bok choy contains 2183 mg vitamin A, .14 mg vitamin B-6, 22 mg vitamin C, 35 mg folic acid and 79 mg calcium. One-half cup cooked Napa cabbage contains 575 mg vitamin A, 9 mg vitamin C and 32 mg folic acid; one-half cup cooked Savoy cabbage has 649 mg vitamin A, 12 mg vitamin C and 34 mg folic acid.

CARROTS: See root vegetables

CAULIFLOWER: Another cruciferous vegetable, cauliflower grows best in cooler weather. The most common variety is white, but it can be found in green and purple varieties also. Look for firm, heavy bunches with no sign of browning. Refrigerate in a plastic bag with as little air as possible for several days. Frozen cauliflower is acceptable in cooking. One-half cup of cooked cauliflower contains 27 mg vitamin C and 27 mg folic acid.

CELERY: Originally a fall vegetable, celery is now available every season. Its most common variety is **Pascal** celery, found in bunched, firm, crisp ribs topped with tender leaves. Its close relative, **celery root** or **celeriac,** is a popular winter vegetable in Europe with a more intense celery flavor. Celery root has a knobby, round, brown-skinned exterior that, once peeled, exposes a pale, crisp, ivory interior. Pascal celery should be firm when purchased, with crisp, unblemished ribs. Its leaves should not be limp. Celery root should be small and firm, with as few knobs as possible. Refrigerate celery and celery root, stored in a plastic bag — celery for two weeks, celery root for one. Best fresh. One-half cup cooked celery contains 99 mg vitamin A and 66 mg calcium. Raw celery root (3.5-oz.) contributes 110 mg calcium to the diet.

CORN: A New World discovery, **sweet corn** is still far more popular here for eating than anywhere else. The essence of summer, corn has an endless variety of hybrids, appearing in yellow, white and a blend of both on the cob. Asian recipes call for **baby corn,** consisting of immature ears of sweet corn. Buy and eat as soon as possible after picking. The green leaves covering the ears should not be dry, the silk should not be withered, the kernels should extend to the top of the ear and moisture should spurt from the kernels when pierced. Keep refrigerated no more than a day. Frozen or canned corn is an acceptable substitution. One-half cup cooked corn contains 178 mg vitamin A.

CUCUMBERS: This ancient vegetable is a member of the gourd family. Available in various sizes, the longest is the **English cucumber,** a variety without seeds

that grows up to two feet. Look for firm, smooth cucumbers. Smaller cucumbers tend to have smaller, less bitter seeds. Avoid any softness or withering. Refrigerate, wrapped in plastic, up to a week and a half. Best fresh or pickled. One-half cup raw cucumber contains 112 mg vitamin A.

EGGPLANT: A member of the nightshade family, this late summer vegetable is really a fruit. The most common eggplant is the large, teardrop-shaped variety with creamy flesh and a deep purple skin. **Japanese eggplant** is much smaller and narrower. **White eggplant** is egg-shaped and gives this vegetable its name. Asian markets feature a wide selection of different green varieties, some as small as cherries. Look for shiny, heavy, firm-skinned eggplants with no soft spots. Store at cool room temperature for a day or so or a bit longer stored in the refrigerator's vegetable crisper. Best fresh. Eggplant contributes minimal vitamins.

FENNEL: A cool-weather vegetable, fennel is primarily grown here and in the Mediterranean. Its most common variety, **Florence fennel,** has celery-like stems with feathery fronds and a broad base. The other variety, **common fennel,** produces fennel seeds. Fennel should be firm and crisp with no brown spots. Store refrigerated, wrapped airtight, for four to five days. Best fresh. One-half cup raw fennel contains 58 mg vitamin A and 22 mg calcium.

GARLIC: A member of the lily family, garlic is an early summer crop grown primarily in this country in California, Texas and Louisiana. Garlic comes with both white and purple skins or as **elephant garlic** with larger cloves and milder flavor. Some markets also offer **green garlic,** which is the immature shoot of the garlic plant before cloves are formed. Store at cool room temperature with air circulation. Available fresh, chopped or minced in refrigerated jars, or dehydrated. While low in vitamins and

minerals, garlic has been attributed with healthful properties for centuries.

GREENS: A broad category of vegetable comprising the edible leaves of plants. A cool-weather crop, varieties include **collard, kale, mustard** and **spinach.** Look for fresh leaves, full of moisture, with no yellowing. Smaller leaves will be more tender. Store airtight in the refrigerator for several days. Best fresh, but frozen spinach works well in cooking. One-half cup cooked collard greens contains 1746 mg vitamin A and 15 mg calcium. One-half cup cooked kale contains 4810 mg vitamin A, 27 mg vitamin C and 31 mg calcium.

One-half cup cooked mustard greens contain 2122 mg vitamin A, 18 mg vitamin C, 51 mg folic acid and 52 mg calcium. One-half cup cooked spinach contains 7371 mg vitamin A, 9 mg vitamin C, .22 mg vitamin B-6, 131 mg folic acid and 122 mg calcium.

LEEKS: Related to the lily, leeks resemble an overgrown green onion with a white, slightly bulbous base and green, leafy top. A favorite in the Mediterranean, leeks favor the cooler months for growing. Look for small, firm, unblemished leeks with crisp-looking stems. Refrigerate loosely wrapped in a plastic bag for four to five days. Best fresh. Leeks contribute minimal vitamins.

LETTUCES: Primarily a cool-weather crop, these leafy vegetables include **Belgian endive, escarole, iceberg, leaf** and **romaine.** Belgian endive is a small, pale, oval head of tightly packed leaves with a slightly bitter flavor. Escarole is part of the same family, with broad leaves in a flatter head; its flavor is milder than Belgian endive. Iceberg lettuce comes in round heads of tightly packed, crunchy leaves with a neutral flavor. Leaf lettuces come in a variety of shapes and color tones, including red-tinted, distinguished by growing from a central stem into a loose bunch. Romaine grows in an elongated bunch, with

crunchy leaves that vary from dark green outside to pale inside. All lettuces should look fresh; avoid limp leaves with brown edges. Refrigerate lettuce, wrapped in a barely damp paper towel, in an airtight plastic bag for several days to a week depending on the variety. Best fresh. Belgian endive and iceberg lettuce contribute minimal vitamins; one-half cup escarole contains 99 mg folic acid and 90 mg calcium. One-half cup leaf lettuce contains 532 mg vitamin A; one-half cup romaine contains 728 mg vitamin A.

MUSHROOMS: This broad category of edible fungi has been grown for consumption since the Greeks and Romans. White mushrooms are cultivated year-round while exotic, or wild, mushrooms appear at different seasons throughout the year depending on the variety. Many

are now under cultivation, making them more accessible. The *Boletus* family of mushrooms is variously called **cèpes, porcini** and **steinpilze** depending on their country of origin. They are widely used in European cooking and are primarily available dried in this country. **Chanterelles** are trumpet-shaped mushrooms whose colors range from golden to orange. They are grown in Europe, the Pacific Northwest and the East Coast. **Portobello** mushrooms are larger versions of the cultivated **crimini** or brown mushroom. Fresh mushrooms should be unbroken and free of moist or discolored spots. Store them in the refrigerator, loosely covered, to allow for air circulation, for several days. Best fresh or dried but canned or frozen may be substituted. Mushrooms contribute minimal vitamins but are a satisfying, low-calorie and fat-free substitute for meat.

OKRA: Popular in the southern United States and in other hot climates, okra is a warm-weather crop. Tapered at one end, okra has ridged sides and an oblong shape. Look for firm, blemish-free pods. Avoid larger, woody pods; the smaller the pod, the more tender it will be. Refrigerate for several days in a plastic bag. Best fresh but frozen is an acceptable substitute in some recipes. One half cup cooked okra contains 411 mg vitamin A, 10 mg vitamin C, 116 mg folic acid and 77 mg calcium.

ONIONS: Related to lilies, this category includes **pearl onions, red onions, scallions** or **green onions** along with the more familiar **yellow** and **white onions.** Depending on the variety, their season extends from spring through the fall months and into winter. Green onions or scallions are harvested immaturely before the base has turned into the familiar large bulb of the dried onion. Pearl onions are small

versions of the larger varieties. Other types include the **Bermuda, Globe, Maui, Spanish, Vidalia** and **Walla Walla onions** with flavors ranging from sweet to sharp. Yellow onions found in supermarkets are often the Bermuda or Spanish with relatively mild flavors. White onions have a silvery skin and are usually quite mild. Fresh, green onions should be crisp; dried onions should be firm. Avoid any with soft spots or molding. Store at cool room temperature with air circulation. Best fresh; some varieties are also available frozen or canned. One-half cup raw green onion contains 193 mg vitamin A and 36 mg calcium; the remainder contribute minimal vitamins.

PARSNIPS: See root vegetables

PEAS: A spring crop, peas are legumes. Their varieties include **English peas** which are normally eaten with shell removed, **sugar snap peas** which are eaten with both pod and pea, and **snow peas** or **pea pods** which are eaten for the pod. Look for fresh, crisp pods with no sign of wilting or spots. The inner pea should be smallish or, in the case of pea pods, virtually nonexistent. Best fresh but frozen may be substituted. One-half cup cooked, shelled peas contains 478 mg vitamin A, .18 mg vitamin B-6, 12 mg vitamin C, 51 mg folic acid and 22 mg calcium; one-half cup cooked edible pod peas contains 105 mg vitamin A, .12 mg vitamin B-6, 39 mg vitamin C and 34 mg calcium.

PEPPERS, SWEET AND HOT: These members of the *Capsicum* family range in flavor from sweet to hot and are a midsummer to early fall crop. Native to the Western Hemisphere, they are used globally. **Bell peppers,** so named because of their shape, start out green; some then ripen to red, yellow, orange and purple. Hot peppers are more often called chiles and come in a wide range of shapes, sizes and colors. Their heat

comes from the seeds and membranes. Smaller chiles are often hotter. The Scoville scale rates the hotness of the pepper by determining the amount of capsaicin the pepper contains. **Anaheim peppers,** also called **New Mexico peppers,** are fairly mild, **jalapeño, chipotle** (smoked jalapeño) and **serrano peppers** are medium-hot. Bottled hot sauce is made from very hot peppers such as **habañero** or **tabasco.** (Names of chiles can vary depending on the regional cuisine, and some change names when dried, so ask questions if in doubt.) Look for

firm, heavy, blemish-free peppers with shiny skins. Refrigerate for up to a week in a plastic bag. One-half cup green sweet peppers contains 316 mg vitamin A, .12 mg vitamin B-6 and 45 mg vitamin C. Red sweet peppers contain 2850 mg vitamin A and 95 mg vitamin C. One hot pepper contains 347 mg vitamin A, .13 mg vitamin B-6 and 109 mg vitamin C. Red varieties contain 4838 mg vitamin A.

POTATOES: Being a member of the nightshade family, potatoes were once thought to be poisonous. Small, immature new potatoes are harvested in the spring and early summer with other varieties available year-round. **Idaho russets** are low in moisture and high in starch, giving them a fluffy texture when cooked. Moist **Yukon Golds** have a buttery color and **red** or **boiling potatoes** have a waxy, moist flesh that is low in starch. Potatoes should be firm, without spots, sprouts or greenish tinge. Store them at cool room temperature, away from light, for one to two weeks. Best fresh. One baked potato without skin contains .47 mg vitamin B-6 and 20 mg vitamin C. One boiled potato without skin contains .4 mg vitamin B-6 and 18 mg vitamin C.

PUMPKIN: See winter squashes

RADISHES: A member of the mustard family, radishes are a sign of spring but can be found year-round. Besides the familiar red, round radish, other varieties range in color from white to black. Shapes also vary such as the elongated, tapered oblong of the **daikon radish.** Radishes should be crisp and not yield when pressed. If sold with leaves attached, they should show no signs of wilting. Refrigerate for four to five days in a plastic bag. Best fresh. Radishes

contribute minimal vitamins.

ROOT VEGETABLES: So named because their edible portion grows beneath the ground, root vegetables are a mainstay of fall and winter cooking. **Beets,** also known as garden beets, are related to Swiss chard and sugar beets. Beets have a round, sweet base and crinkly leaves; both are edible. Besides the normal deep red, look

for yellow, white and **chioggia,** or candy cane, varieties. **Carrots** and **parsnips** are members of the parsley family and share a common sweetness of flavor. **Turnips** also have a mildly sweet flavor with a peppery finish. Look for firm root vegetables, never limp; the smaller vegetables are often more tender. Store beets trimmed of their greens. All root vegetables may be stored in the refrigerator in a plastic bag for up to two weeks. Beets may keep a bit longer, and turnips also store well at cool room temperature. All are best fresh. One-half cup cooked beets contains 68 mg folic acid and

14 mg calcium; one-half cup cooked carrots contains 152 mg vitamin A, .19 mg vitamin B-6 and 24 mg calcium. One-half cup cooked parsnips contains 10 mg vitamin C, 45 mg folic acid and 29 mg calcium. One-half cup cooked turnips contains 9 mg vitamin C and 17 mg calcium. (See also potatoes and sweet potatoes.)

SHALLOTS: A relative of the onion, shallots are an early summer crop but available year-round. They grow in bulbs with off-white or slightly purple flesh covered with brown, paper-thin skins. Look for firm bulbs without sprouts. Store at cool room temperature with ample air circulation. Best fresh. One tablespoon of raw shallots contains 1248 mg vitamin A.

SPINACH: See greens

SUMMER SQUASHES: As their name implies, these members of the gourd family are a summer crop. Marked by thin outer skin

and tiny, edible seeds, this category includes **pattypan, yellow** or **crookneck squash** and **zucchini.** Pattypans have a spaceship-like shape with scalloped edges, and range in

color from pale green to yellow. Yellow or crookneck squash are so named because of their color and neck shape that ends in a bulb-like base. Zucchini are narrow and cylindrical with green skins and creamy flesh. Purchase smaller rather than larger summer squashes. All should be firm and blemish-free. Store refrigerated in a plastic bag for three to four days. One-half cup cooked pattypan squash contains 77 mg vitamin A and 14 mg calcium; one-half cup of cooked yellow squash contains 258 mg vitamin A and 24 mg calcium. One-half cup cooked zucchini contains 216 mg vitamin A and 12 mg calcium.

SWEET POTATOES: Sweet potatoes are not really potatoes, nor are the paler or more orangey varieties sold in the United States really yams. Rather, these starchy tubers are related to the morning glory. A cool-weather crop, sweet potatoes should be firm and blemish-free. Stored under cool, dry and dark conditions, they may keep for several weeks but are best if used promptly, within a week of purchase. One-half cup of cooked sweet potato contains 316 mg vitamin A, .27 mg vitamin B-6, 28 mg vitamin C and 34 mg calcium.

TOMATOES: A member of the nightshade family, the tomato is a summer crop. Spread to Europe from the New World, the tomato was originally feared to be poisonous. Tomatoes come in an amazing variety of shapes and colors, ranging from vivid red globes to yellow pear shapes, with a full spectrum in between including green-striped and purple. The most common varieties include the round **beefsteak tomato** that's perfect for slicing, the pear-shaped **Roma** or **plum tomato** with lots of flesh and fewer seeds and the tiny **cherry tomato** used in salads or with dips. Look for heirloom

varieties grown from heritage seeds that have not been hybridized. Tomatoes should be heavy and slightly yielding with good color. Store at room temperature for several days. Best fresh or canned when out of season. One-half cup of cooked tomatoes contains 892 mg vitamin A, .11 mg vitamin B-6 and 27 mg vitamin C.

WINTER SQUASHES: These members of the gourd family have harder skins and seeds than their summer cousins, and come into their own in the fall and winter. Common varieties include **acorn**

squash, shaped like its namesake with a green skin, and **butternut squash** with a narrower neck, bulbous base and pale, slightly rosy-beige skin. **Hubbard squash** are large and bumpy while **spaghetti squash** have yellow skins with pasta-like flesh. **Pumpkins,** a mainstay of the early Colonial diet, are known for their round, orange exterior. Smaller pumpkins are tastier than their larger varieties. All winter squash should be heavy and blemish-free with hard exteriors. Store at cool room temperature in a dark place. Squash are available fresh, frozen or canned. One-half cup baked acorn squash contains 437 mg vitamin A, .2 mg vitamin B-6, 11 mg vitamin C and 12 mg calcium; one-half cup baked butternut squash contains 7141 mg vitamin A, .13 mg vitamin B-6, 115 mg vitamin C and 42 mg calcium. One-half cup cooked hubbard squash contains 4726 mg vitamin A, .12 mg vitamin B-6, 8 mg vitamin C and 12 mg calcium; one-half cup cooked spaghetti squash contains 86 mg vitamin A and 16 mg calcium. One-half cup of cooked pumpkin contains 1320 mg vitamin A and 18 mg calcium.

SOURCES

Here is a listing of possible mail order and Internet sources
for hard-to-find ingredients.

Adriana's Caravan
409 Vanderbilt Street
Brooklyn, NY 11218
1 (800) 316-0820

www.adrianascaravan.com

Source for international ingredients,
including North African

Joie de Vivre
P. O. Box 875
Modesto, CA 95353
1 (800) 648-8854

Source for French ingredients

Coyote Café General Store
132 West Water Street
Santa Fe, NM 87501
1 (800) 866-4695

www.coyotecafeatmgm.com

Source for southwestern ingredients

Pacific Island Market
4111 Mexico Road
St. Peters, MO 63376
1 (877) 274-2639

www.asiamex.com

Source for Asian and Mexican
ingredients

Dean and Deluca
560 Broadway
New York, NY 10012
1 (800) 221-7714

www.dean-deluca.com

Source for gourmet foods

Penzeys
P. O. Box 933
Muskego, WI 53150
1 (800) 741-7787

www.penzeys.com

Source for spices and herbs

BIBLIOGRAPHY

These materials have been a source of inspiration and
information in writing this book.

Fletcher, Janet. *Fresh from the Farmers' Market.*
San Francisco: Chronicle Books, 1997.

Greene, Bert. *Greene on Greens.*
New York: Workman Publishing, 1984.

Herbst, Sharon Tyler. *The New Food Lover's Companion.*
New York: Barrons, 1995.

Madison, Deborah. *Vegetarian Cooking for Everyone.*
New York: Broadway Books, 1997.

Pennington, Jean A. *Bowes and Church's Food Values of
Portions Commonly Used.* Philadelphia: Lippincott, 1998.

Sinclair, Charles. *International Dictionary of Food and
Cooking.* Great Britain: Peter Collin Publishing, 1998.

RECIPE INDEX

This index lists every recipe in Vegetable Creations *by name. If you're looking for a specific recipe but can't recall the exact name, refer to the General Index that starts on page 153.*

GENERAL INDEX

There are several ways to use this helpful index. First — you can find recipes by name. If you don't know a recipe's specific name but recall a main vegetable ingredient, look under that heading and all the recipes using that ingredient will be listed; scan for the recipe you want. If you have a vegetable in mind and want to find a great recipe for it, look under that ingredient heading as well to find a list of recipes to choose from. Finally — you can use this general index to find a summary of the recipes in each chapter of the book (appetizers, side dishes, salads, etc.).